W9-CIJ-549

BATIK
for
Artists and Quilters

Contents

Photo by William Zinner

Sand Dunes (detail), by Eloise Piper.

*This book is dedicated with love
to my mother, Martha Fort*

Summer Meadow, by Eloise Piper, 90"w x 52"h.

Foreword
An Approach to a Rare Artistry

by Donald Miller

The Western art world is fortunate to have, at last in this book, a highly readable and comprehensive approach to the art of batik.

I have known the work of Eloise Piper, an outstanding batik artist, for more than twenty-five years. It was my privilege when Eloise lived in Pittsburgh to mention her often in my reviews of exhibitions for the excellence of her batik creations. They resembled landscape paintings of beautiful imaginary scenes — more than the simple decorative patterns many people think of as batik.

Like Eloise, I had failed to find an explanation of batik as an art form beyond the mere description in an encyclopedia. For me, the pressures of daily journalism deadlines pushed the matter to the back of my mind where it seldom resurfaced. But Eloise's interest as a professional artist in this medium only grew deeper. The excellent results of her personal inquiries and trial-and-error methods are here before you. This book is the result of them — and Eloise's zeal to bring that knowledge to a wider public.

Having participated in many arts and crafts as a youth, I am deeply impressed with how Eloise, a true teacher, not only found her way through a maize of techniques and styles but was also able to bring this material together in a trenchant way. It will be valuable to the experienced batikist as well as the beginner.

Like many other arts, batik is quite demanding of the artists' skills. But the effort is worth the exciting results, if one is able to realize them with freshness and verve. Eloise Piper long ago perfected this elusive art and now, after several years of writing this book, shares that knowledge with you.

Other than writing about her and others' work, my most direct experience with batik occurred a few years ago when I purchased for myself two shirts — one short-sleeve, one long-sleeve — made in quilt-style from antique Thai fabrics. My wife Bette also chose several garments made of similar batik squares, some pieced, some appliqued.

Although, like Eloise, I never enjoyed the typical crude psychedelic T-shirts of the 1970s, I love my loose-

Photo by Bette Weinbrenner

fitting shirts that have cooled me through many a day. Sometimes, though, the old fabric squares pull apart in small rents. Darning them, I think, only improves them, if indeed anyone notices.

In style the patterns in the shirts are related only by nationality, yet they possess a beauty that I never tire of. As with Bette and her skirt, slacks, and bolero, I hope to wear my batiks indefinitely. That's how they have affected me.

But more than that, I see Eloise's glowing batik land-scapes in my mind as easily as I did twenty-five years ago on gallery walls in Pittsburgh. Her gorgeous compositions were, ironically enough, redolent with the shimmering colors she has come to know while living in Southern California. And their fineness was always of a high order. That says much for her unique creativity as an artist. It also indicates what one can learn from Eloise Piper in this long-needed volume.

Introduction

"Here, see what you can do with this." With those words Mary Auld, my *Materials and Processes* professor at Carnegie Tech, handed me a tool that resembled a small teapot on a stout handle. "What is it?" I asked. "It's a tjanting. It is used for batik," she replied. I slipped it into my green tackle box, alongside all the other tools of an art student's trade, and rushed off to my next class. Later, while at the library, I remembered the odd-looking tool and looked up the word batik in the dictionary.

Webster's dictionary tersely reads:
batik\ be'tek, 'bat-ik\ n {Malay} (1880) 1a: an Indonesian method of hand-printing textiles by coating with wax the parts not to be dyed, b: a design so executed, 2: a fabric printed by batik.

Photo by Bernice Meissner

Tjantings.

Not much information there. But it did sound like an interesting craft, so I moved on to other references. My initial search through books and magazines turned up a scant amount of background history and very little practical information. I did find an old National Geographic magazine article that showed Javanese women filling their tjantings with wax shavings and holding them over a flame to melt the wax before applying it to the fabric.

At home I dutifully filled the tjanting with candle shavings and held it over the candle flame only to have great black smudges of soot drip off the tjanting and onto the fabric. So much for that tradition! I then tried melting the wax in a tin can set on a hotplate. This was equally disastrous, for the wax began to smoke and then suddenly leapt into flame. I went back to the drawing board with singed eyebrows and my hair firmly secured out of harm's way with a scarf. The next effort, a makeshift double boiler with a jug of water near at hand, finally proved successful in melting the wax.

My early attempts using paraffin, old sheets and over-the-counter commercial dyes were exercises in forbearance and determination. Drips and dribbles poured from the tjanting's spout, the waxed fabric adhered itself firmly to the tabletop, damaging my patience as well as the design when I pulled it loose. The over-the-counter dyes washed out or rapidly faded, and ironing the wax out on newspapers transferred inky print markings all over the finished batiks. To make matters worse, the wax left a greasy-looking residue along the borders of the ironed designs. This was not easy!

But something in this magical process kept me going. Maybe it was the fluid ribbon of wax that flowed from the spout, transforming my mind's images into concrete designs. Maybe it was the way the design bonded with the fabric in an instantaneous melding of process and product, or the challenge of the overlapping dyes whose rich, enigmatic colors were revealed only after all the work was completed. It was probably all of these factors, plus the intrigue and challenge of a new and uncharted venture. I had found my medium! And so began my long odyssey into the ancient art of batik.

August (detail), by Eloise Piper.

And indeed it was my medium. I found myself working whenever I could — after class, after work, after the children's bedtimes, and once the children reached school age, on a regular daily schedule. It was an exciting challenge to hone and perfect the technical skills of the craft. If I used five colors in a particular batik, the next would have ten, the next fifteen. The later works had up to 40 emersion dyed, overlapping colors. I soon replaced the old cotton sheets with a variety of silks and the fugitive over-the-counter dyes gave way to special mail-order batik dyes. Eventually, a designated workstation replaced the dining room table. When the artwork began to take over the entire house, I moved the operation to a large, sunny studio a few miles away.

As I developed the skills needed to create the images in my mind's eye, motifs of butterflies, birds, suns and stars, flowers and fruit flowed from the tjanting. Each image led to a continued series of images that explored all the variations of that particular motif. Sometimes work on a series would last for weeks, sometimes for years. Early imagery was often incorporated into the more complex work of the later years. The early bouquets of flowers became the intricate patterns of meadows and forests. Random, experimental textures developed into cobblestones, bricks and shingles of detailed cityscapes.

My years as an art educator stood me in good stead when I was asked to teach in-service training classes for public school art teachers. There was surprising interest in this ancient craft, and these intensive workshops soon became popular with art centers, craft schools and colleges, providing a wonderful exchange of information, creative energy, and inspiration. I often thought of putting the workshop into book form but three children, graduate school, studio time, one or two solo shows each year, group exhibitions, teaching, and years of renovating an old house left little time for that venture. By 1980 I was ready to move on to other media and I put down my tjanting to take up brush, clay, and camera. I kept the idea of a book on batik in the back of my mind, but my writing turned instead to prose, poetry, and finally to books on surface design and dollmaking.

The popularity of batik ebbed and flowed. The splurge of crude, crackled T-shirts of the 60's love generation and the pillows and wall hangings of the home-crafters of the 70's faded into obscurity. The following decade showed little interest in the medium except for a handful of dedicated artists who continued the tradition, each working in relative isolation from the other.

Batik re-emerged in the 1990s as a fine art medium and a sophisticated surface design method for haute couture as well as for mass-produced commercial fabrics and homecraft projects. While there was a renewed interest in batik, there still seemed to be very little current information about it. Once again I began to dream of a book based on the workshops, one that would present the incredible artistry of batik along with a practical how-to craft guide. This book is the result of that dream. Batik artists from all over the world have joined in the project, sharing their special techniques and samples of their work. I hope you are awed, inspired, and informed

Factory Town
by Eloise Piper,
24"w x 32"h.

Photo by William Zinner

by this volume and that it gives you a greater appreciation of the art and craft of batik.

This book is for anyone who is intrigued with the creation of art and curious about the production of craft. If you are interested in pursuing the craft, you will find all the information you need to get started. If you are merely looking for a good read and lots of pictures, I hope you will find that here too. I've tried to make the text accessible, and it is richly illustrated with hundreds of photographs. The works of many artists, each with a truly unique approach to the medium, are shown along with step-by-step photo sequences of many waxing and dyeing methods. Throughout the book there is an emphasis on the safe handling of supplies and equipment. There is also a bibliography, an index, and a detailed materials list.

But let's go back to the beginnings and for that turn to chapter one for a description of the craft and a brief history.

1

What is Batik?

Batik, *a Javanese word meaning* wax writing, *is based on the process of* resist, *one of the oldest known methods of applying design to surface. Portions of fabric are coated with melted wax, rice paste, or some other non water-soluble substance, and the fabric is then submerged in or painted with dye. The dye does not penetrate the areas of fabric that are covered with resist and they remain their original color. When the dyed fabric is dry, the process can be repeated. Designs can be created from a single waxing and dyeing or from any number of layers. I have used up to forty dye-baths to create some of my large batik paintings. The wax can be removed and reapplied periodically throughout the process or after completion of the final layer of wax and dye. After the batik is completed and the resist is removed, the fabric is steamed or ironed to permanently set the color.*

Cracks and veins can be a part of the final batik design. The type of resist that is used, the temperature of the dye bath, and the amount of handling the fabric receives all play a part in determining this textural effect. Brittle resist substances such as paraffin, or paraffin mixed with resin, produce the veining that is often seen in batik. This random crackling can be further enhanced by deliberate manipulation of the

Photo by Edward Kessler

Cotton fabric, **courtesy of Salsa Fabrics.**

Commercially printed cotton made to look like traditional batik. Motif created from thousands of tiny, evenly spaced dots.

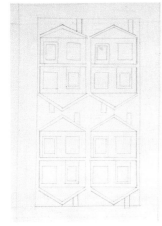
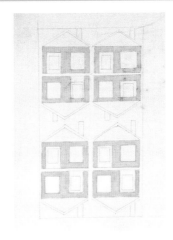
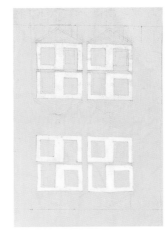

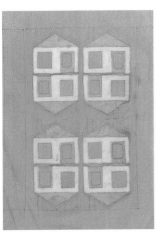

First Row (left to right)

1   Design drawn on white fabric.
2   First layer of wax applied.
3   Fabric dyed yellow.
4   Second layer of wax applied.

Second Row

5   Fabric dyed orange.
6   Third layer of wax applied.
7   Fabric dyed tan.
8   Fourth layer of wax applied.

Third Row

9   Fabric dyed brown.
10 Wax removed from fabric.

Photos by Edward Kessler

coated surface, making the direction and density of the cracks part of the planned design, not just accidental occurrences.

Bees wax or other more pliable resists, along with careful handling of the fabric and warming the dye baths allow even the largest of coated areas to remain free of veining. The absence of cracks enhances the intricacy of a complex, multi-colored design.

Veined or smooth, simple or complex, one color or multi-colored, batik is an amazing and versatile surface embellishment. Its roots are in antiquity, its history spans the ages, and it has reemerged today, both as a

fine art and as a unique surface embellishment for the fabric, fashion, quilt, and crafting industries.

Origins

The exact origin of batik is unknown. It is thought that over 35,000 years ago prehistoric cave dwellers pressed berry juice through the holes of insect-chewed leaves to create the earliest known resist patterns. Stenciling, wax-resist ceramic glazing, ikat weaving, tie-dyeing, katazome, and batik are some of the many resist methods to have sprung from this early beginning. Remnants of resist-embellished fabrics have been found in ancient Egypt, Peru, China, India, and Africa indicating that each culture developed its resist crafts independent of the others. The people of Indonesia, particularly Java, took the resist method as their own, named it and perfected it into what we know today as batik.

Traditional Javanese batik was an exacting and painstaking procedure. All parts of the design except the areas that were to receive the darkest of the colors (usually a deep blue) were carefully waxed, first on one side of the fabric and then on the other. The fabric was then dipped in the dye vat. This was done with great care so as not to break the wax — for a design with cracks or fissures was considered inferior. After the fabric was dyed and dried the wax was scraped off the surface and the fabric was boiled to remove all remaining traces of wax residue. This procedure of wax, dye, scrape and boil was carefully repeated for each of the other colors in the design. Batik with overlapping colors, like those with cracks and crazing, was considered substandard. In fact it was considered to be of such poor quality that is was often destroyed.

Top: *Jakarta*, by Lauren Rosenblum, 60"w x 80"h.

Contemporary quilt design is reminiscent of a traditional Javanese sarong.

Left: *Sun Storms*
by Joyce Dewsbury, 24"w x 24"h.

Gutta resist and hand painted dyes on silk.

The Malay culture developed a batik tradition consisting of two main design styles, symmetrical all-over geometric motifs and flowing freehand patterns. Some motifs were kept within a family and passed down from generation to generation, much like the patterns and colors of plaids that identify various Scottish clans. Others were considered forbidden designs and were designated exclusively for use by the Javanese royal court. Colors varied according to region. The southern coastal area preferred dark blues, browns, and pure whites, while the inland region used yellows, tans and creamy off-whites. As with the forbidden design motifs, particular colors and color combinations were restricted for use by royalty and those of noble birth.

Javanese batik was also influenced by the many foreign cultures that left their mark on Indonesia. The traditional designs became interwoven with Asian, European, and Arabic sensibilities. In the northern regions, bold and brightly colored designs of fish and fowl, fruits and flowers, birds and beasts, reflected the design preferences of the Chinese. Northern trade routes to India, established in the first century A.D., brought Hindu and Buddhist cultures to the Malay Peninsula. Images of nature became stylized rather than realistic, with flowing lines and rounded shapes. Islam was introduced to Java around the twelfth century and soon native design motifs incorporated Islamic abstract geometric patterns. In some regions the Islamic taboo against representation of the human figure was also embraced.

The designs of these diverse cultures included social and spiritual symbolism, which influenced not only the motifs but also the usage of the finished fabric. Royal ceremonies as well as births, deaths, circumcisions and weddings each

Cedars Period, by Arnelle Dow, 24"w x 40"h.

utilized special fabrics decorated with pre-designated symbols. For example, peaches represented fruitfulness and images of the fruit were often used to decorate wedding sarongs.

By the eleventh or twelfth century, the Javanese had turned this unique and intricate art form into a small but thriving industry. They invented the tjanting and used it with amazing dexterity to apply the temperamental hot wax to the fabric. It was the women, trained from childhood, who applied the wax designs to fabric. Men dyed the fabric and then removed the wax and steam set the dyes. There was even a period of time when batik was decreed a craft to be practiced exclusively by the women of royalty.

Colors and methods of application changed little over time until the fourteenth century when Dutch and Portuguese traders introduced batik to Europe. This created a demand for the exotically patterned fabric far beyond the limited supply that Java's royal ladies and independent crafters could produce. An expanded industry of skilled artisans emerged and they, in turn, developed a variety of faster production methods. Tjantings were created with two or three spouts that could quickly wax parallel lines and multiple dots. Tjaps, stamps carved from wood and embedded with metal, were used to press the wax pattern onto the fabric in far less time than the tedious hand method of waxing. Careful use of these stamping tools could quickly and efficiently produce batik-patterned fabrics in great quantity.

European dyes brought an exuberant palette of bright hues to batik. No longer limited to local sources for the natural dyes and no longer restricted by royalty and symbolism, the batik crafter applied these bright colors in new ways. Areas of fabric were outlined with walls of wax and the fabric then hand painted to create color arrangements not possible with traditional dying methods. Combinations of hand painting, walling in of color, and traditional immersion dyeing added to the variety of production methods. Batik was now a major export business and other countries began to develop their own batik industries. India, Africa, Europe, and China each produced fabric in their unique design styles. There was even a time when the Javanese imported European-made batik to satisfy the demand for this popular fabric.

Each following century brought its influence to this ancient art form. In the seventeenth century the popularity of the Netherlands's delftware created a demand for chro-

Photo by artist

Photo by artist

Above: *Monday, Monday,* by Rosi Robinson, 88cm x 64cm.

Opposite: *Winter Creek,* by Karen Perrine, 63"w x 39.5"h.

Wax resist and hand painted dyes on cotton sateen embellished with pigment and knit mesh. Machine pieced and quilted.

matic blue and white batiks, often similar in pattern to the famous tinglaze ware. The eighteenth century baroque movement brought extravagant curves and monumental motifs to batik designs, followed by the rococo's exaggerated flourishes. A new palette of colors was introduced to batik with the discovery of aniline dyes in 1856. The late nineteenth century crafts movement in Europe, responding to the industrial revolution's influence on the arts and building trades, rediscovered batik as a surface design method for decorating wall-coverings, upholstery fabric, and draperies, as well as for clothing embellishment. In the early decades of the twentieth century, the organic art nouveau designs, followed by geometric art deco motifs, also found expression in the fluid wax and dye of batik.

Resurgence of the hand crafts movement in the 1960s and 1970s gave new life to batik. Along with tie-dye and macramé, batik represented the epitome of that "do-it-yourself" era. Simple designs with lots of cracks and crazing emblazoned the love generation's T-shirts and shoulder bags. Today a rebirth of batik can be seen in the paintings created by artists who choose batik as their medium and the many sophis-ticated decorative projects of the home crafters. Batik and discharge techniques have become a popular means for embellishing and personalizing quilts as well. Resist-designed fabrics can also be found on runways of the haute couture industry and in the commercial yardage at your local fabric store.

In Summary

Batik is truly an art and craft for all times and all seasons. No matter when, where or how it is produced, it is an enduring art form that is admired for its intricate beauty and the unique and exacting skill utilized in its creation.

Equipment, Tools & Materials

It does not take a vast array of specialty supplies or a lot of elbowroom to get started with batik. You can set up shop at one end of the kitchen table using the simplest of supplies. To begin you will need an appliance to melt the wax, a frame, thumbtacks, fabric, and a brush or two. You will also need cold water dyes, a few basic dyeing supplies, newsprint and an iron. As you increase your skills you may want to add to these basic supplies and find a more permanent workstation — one that does not need to be cleared away before every meal.

This chapter provides you with a comprehensive list of batik equipment, tools, and materials followed by a brief discussion of the key items, as well as suggestions for setting up a workstation. But first, a few words about safety.

Safety First

Batik requires a number of materials that can be hazardous to your health if not handled properly. This should not hinder your exploration into the medium, just use common sense and follow a few basic safety precautions. Begin by keeping children, pets, and your hands away from the hot wax and electrical equipment. Make sure the electrical cords and

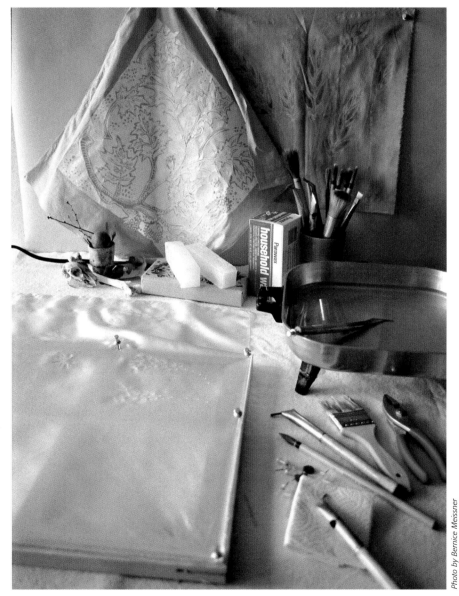

The workstation.

Photo by Bernice Meissner

plugs are in perfect working order and that they are not stretched across the path of traffic.

Follow all safety procedures when handling hot wax, discharge pastes, chemicals, dyes, and wax-removal equipment. Masks protect against the hazard of inhaling the poisonous dyes and fumes and having them absorbed through the mucous membranes. Gloves prevent poisons from being absorbed through the skin. Wear both when working with dyes and chemicals.

Make sure all foodstuffs and kitchen utensils are put away and cover the work area to prevent the dye from contaminating the surface. Damp paper towels under the mixing area will pick up any spills and prevent them from becoming airborne. If you are using fiber-reactive dyes, avoid working in the kitchen. Instead, dye the batik outside, in the garage, or at a utility sink. Use an exhaust fan to help remove airborne particles and fumes when you are dyeing and ironing the batik indoors.

Photo by Lenore Davis

Supply List

Don't be intimidated by this long list of equipment, tools, and materials. You will not need everything on the list to begin working in batik and many of the items that you will need are ordinary household objects that require no special purchase. Others are inexpensive and easily found in your local grocery, craft shop, or

---

SUPPLY LIST

Drawing Supplies
Pencils and pens
Sketch book

Waxing Equipment
Electric frying pan
(Or hot plate and double boiler)
Wooden frame
Thumbtacks and pushpins
Drop cloth

Waxing Tools
Tjantings
Brushes
Incising tools
Stamping tools

Waxing Materials
Paraffin*
Bees wax*
(Or other resist substances)
Fabrics*

Dyeing Equipment
Large non-reactive dyeing container
Plastic clothesline and clothespins
Non-reactive storage and mixing jars

Dyeing Tools
Non-reactive measuring cups, stirrers, and spoons
Non-reactive fine-mesh strainer and cheese cloth
Non-reactive funnel

Dyeing Materials
Acid dyes*, salt and white household vinegar * OR
Fiber-reactive dyes*
Fiber-reactive additives*
(Urea, Calgon, Calsolene oil, Soda ash)
Sodium alginate (thickener)*
Synthropol (detergent)*
Rubber gloves and face mask*

Wax Removal Supplies
Newspapers*
Unprinted newsprint*
Iron

---

* expendable supplies

hardware store. Also, the majority of equipment and tools are a one-time purchase. Only the items listed under materials and marked with an asterisk are expendable and must be replenished as needed. Look for these supplies at your local art supply shop, fabric outlet, and hardware store, or check for mail order supply sources on the Internet.

Drawing Supplies

SKETCHBOOK

Keep a sketchbook to record your design ideas. This doesn't have to be anything fancy. Sketchbooks come in many sizes, shapes and papers, and can be purchased at art supply shops, bookstores or card shops.

You don't have to be a trained artist to produce imaginative designs. Everyone is born with abundant creativity that can be developed with a little nurturing, practice, and inspiration. Inspiration for your designs can be found in the natural world and in the fertile regions of your imagination. Sometimes it's just a matter of seeing familiar objects in a new way. For instance, examine a leaf. Look at its shape and at the pattern of the veins and stem. A single leaf, or just a portion of a leaf, can be used to create a variety of interesting batik patterns. A geometric shape, a simple household object, or even a telephone doodle all can be the start of an imaginative design.

Waxing Equipment

ELECTRIC FRYING PAN

The safest way to melt the wax is with an electric frying pan. The wax can be placed directly into the pan with no need of a double boiler. The adjustable thermostat assures the correct temperature of wax and the squat design prevents the pan from tipping over. Make sure the thermostat is in working order and that the cord is unfrayed and securely attached to the plug.

HOT PLATE & DOUBLE BOILER

A hot plate coupled with a double boiler can also be used to melt the wax. This is a more hazardous method because of the exposed coils of the hotplate and the possibility of boiling away the water. Keep a large jug of water near at hand and refill the pan every twenty minutes or so. Never leave the hotplate unattended, even for a few minutes.

Pakistan, by Annie Phillips, 36"w x 48"h.

Islands From the Sky
by Mary Edna Fraser.

The artist uses saw horses to support long lengths of fabric during the waxing and dyeing processes.

FRAMES

A frame is used to hold the fabric taut and to keep it up off the tabletop while the wax is being applied. It should be made of soft wood to allow pushpins or thumbtacks to penetrate easily. The size and thickness of the frame is determined by the size of the fabric to be waxed. For smaller batiks use a frame the full size of the fabric to prevent unnecessary pinholes from marring the interior of the design. You can build a small frame from stretcher bars — the same kind that artists use to stretch canvas. They are inexpensive, come in a wide variety of lengths, and are precut and notched to fit together easily. Small wooden wedges called keys fit into the notched corners to keep them at right angles. Look for stretcher bars and keys in your local art supply store.

Larger works require a frame of greater depth than shallow stretcher bars to prevent the heavy waxed fabric from sagging down to the work surface. Build a frame from two by twos. When possible use a frame the width of the fabric and the depth of

your reach when seated at the work-table. Corner joints can be either simple butt joints or beveled at 45° angles.

DROP CLOTH

Protect your work surface with a piece of clean, washable fabric or a length of heavy paper such as brown wrapping paper or shelving paper. Avoid using inky newspapers that might smudge your hands and your work and also avoid slippery, flammable plastic covers. Pre-sewn fabric drop cloths are available in paint and hardware stores.

Waxing Tools

BRUSHES

Brushes are the most basic tools used to apply wax to a surface. They are useful for covering large solid areas and for creating shapes, lines and large dots. Brushes are also handy for resealing previously waxed areas that become eroded from repeated handling.

It is often a trial and error process that leads to finding just the right brush for a particular waxing job. Broad, flat brushes are best for large solid areas, while round brushes that taper to a narrow point allow for maximum control when creating fine lines and small intricate shapes. Select wooden-handle brushes with tightly secured bristles that will not loosen when exposed to the hot wax. Natural bristles are able to withstand the high temperature of the wax better than synthetic ones which tend to curl or melt at high temperatures. Wooden handles do not transmit heat and long handles prevent accidental burns from contact with the hot wax.

Japanese watercolor brushes and calligraphy brushes, both made of boar bristles secured to a bamboo handle, are ideal for the application of wax. They are modestly priced and come in a wide range of shapes and sizes. Calligraphy brushes with fine, tapered points are sold in different size circumferences and lengths. Broad, flat watercolor brushes range in widths of a fraction of an inch to four inches or more. There are also brushes called hake brushes, constructed of a number of small calligraphy brushes aligned in a row and bound together with twine. These are ideal for broad sweeping lines. Flat brushes and foam brushes can also be notched to create bands of parallel lines.

Once a brush has been dipped in wax, a coating of wax remains in the bristles. This coating hardens as it dries, leaving the brush wax-coated and stiff. When the brush is reheated

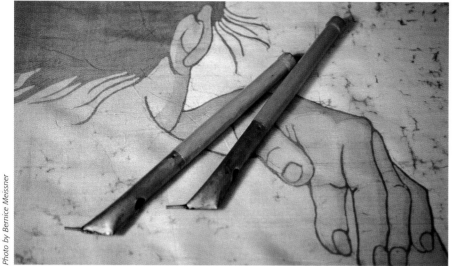

tjanting is filled with melted wax and the hot wax is drawn onto the fabric from the narrow spout. The hot wax penetrates the fabric, sealing the entire thickness of the cloth. When the wax in the tjanting begins to cool, the tjanting must be emptied, reheated, and refilled with hot wax. The working intervals between refillings are usually no more than a few seconds to a few minutes.

Tjanting designs vary from the mass-produced tubular style with one spout, to elaborate tools with two or more drawing spouts. Commercially available tjantings come in three sizes, small, medium and large. The size refers to the diameter of the spout. The narrowest spout is the one used to draw intricate lines and dots. The medium and large size tools are useful for drawing bold patterns and for waxing large solid areas. Multiple spouted tools are useful for drawing precisely spaced parallel lines and dots. These hard-to-find tools are often custom made for specific designs.

Above: Tjantings on *Sleeping Figure* (detail), by Eloise Piper.

Left: *Mythological Bird* by Riki Kölbl Nelson, 25"w x 25"h.

A tjanting was used to create precisely placed dots of wax.

STAMPING TOOLS

Stamping tools called *tjaps* are used to apply the wax onto the fabric. They were created by the Javanese as a shortcut to the laborious waxing methods of tjanting and brush. Some stamps are constructed from a block of wood and thin strips of copper sheeting. A linear design is carved into the surface of the wood. Thin strips of copper are then imbedded into the lines, with up to one inch of metal protruding from the surface. Other stamps are made entirely of metal. A sturdy handle is attached to the back of the stamp. The stamp is dipped into melted wax, heating the copper strips and coating them with the wax. It is then pressed onto fabric, discharging the wax into the cloth. This process is repeated to create borders, all-over patterns, and medallion designs.

in melted wax the film melts and the brush becomes pliable again. This wax film can be removed with mineral spirits, but for all practical purposes it is best to use the selected brushes exclusively for batik, thus avoiding the use of caustic solvents.

TJANTINGS

A trough made from a split length of narrow bamboo is the earliest known tool specifically created for applying melted wax to fabric. Over the cen-

turies, this crude wax applicator evolved into the highly efficient tool called a *tjanting.* The name, derived from the Javanese word *tjap,* meaning to dot, refers to the precise way in which the wax can be applied to the fabric.

This ingenious tool resembles a small, narrow-spouted teapot secured to a long wooden handle. The reservoir is usually made of copper or brass to best retain enough heat to keep the wax fluid for short intervals. The reservoir of the

Photo by Bernice Meissner

Commercial batik designed by Kathy Engle for Hoffman California Fabrics.

Tjap-stamped and hand dyed cotton.

The size of the tjaps range from small stamps of a few inches in width used for small designs and borders to one-foot wide blocks that can cover larger portions of fabric with one application. The overall shape of the stamp is planned to allow the repeated stampings to dovetail seamlessly together. The design motifs on the stamp must also be planned to allow for this seamless repeat.

Wax can also be stamped onto fabric with non-traditional objects. The end of a bamboo brush dipped into wax and pressed onto fabric creates circles, the tines of a fork form short parallel lines. Cookie cutters, bent lengths of stiff wire, corks, nailheads, and blocks of wood covered with felt are just a few of the objects that can be used to stamp unique wax designs onto fabric.

INCISING TOOLS

Delicate linear patterns, sometimes called sgraffito, can be created within solidly waxed areas of fabric. Lines are scraped or carved into the wax with a variety of pointed tools, exposing the fabric beneath. The fabric is then dyed; allowing the exposed areas to pick up the color. Dental tools, knitting needles, ice picks, and nails all can be used as incising tools. Whatever tool you use, special care must be taken not to cut or tear the fibers when incising the lines.

Waxing Materials

PARAFFIN

Paraffin is the least expensive and most available of the resist media. It is an opaque white petroleum-based product commonly used to seal canning jars and can be found in grocery and hardware stores. You can also find paraffin with the candle-making supplies at most craft stores. It is usually packaged in four quarter-pound bars to a box, much like butter. Paraffin melts to a clear liquid at a low temperature and the melted wax penetrates most fabrics. It hardens to a brittle surface that can be easily manipulated to form the cracks and crazing that is so typical of batik.

BEES WAX

Bees wax is a natural substance produced by honeybees to build the hexagonal combs, or cells, in which they store honey and eggs. Pure beeswax is deep yellow ochre in color and has a strong honey fragrance. It melts at a higher temperature

Photo by Ned Pratt

Lily Diptych (detail), by Diana Dabinett.
Gutta resist and hand painted dyes on silk.

times before pouring the clean wax into a shallow pan to cool. Break the firm sheet of wax into small pieces and store in a clean plastic bag.

MICROCRYSTALLINE

Sometimes called sticky wax, this petroleum-based product is an inexpensive substitute for bees wax. It can be combined with paraffin in varying amounts or used by itself for crack-free designs.

COLD RESIST

A thin paste of wheat or rice flour and water can be used to form a cold resist. Add a drop of glycerin to the mixture to make it pliable when dry. Apply the paste to the undyed portion of the fabric with brush, spoon, pastry bag, or palette knife. When the paste is thoroughly dry, the fabric can be submerged in dye or dye can be painted on the surface with a soft brush. After the dye has dried the paste is scraped off the surface of the fabric. Cold resists are ideal for use in school situations where the hot wax and electrical equipment might pose a hazard to children.

COMMERCIAL RESISTS

There are many commercial resist products that can be used to block out areas of a design. Gels, called guttas, come in both solvent and water bases. These clear liquid gels are often packaged in squeeze bottles and can be applied directly onto the fabric from the bottle's thin

than paraffin and is extremely pliable when cooled to room temperature. Bees wax can be added to the paraffin to make a less brittle resist coating. Experiment with the proportion of bees wax to paraffin to find the right flexibility for a particular project. Use pure bees wax for extremely large pieces that are to remain vein-free.

Bees wax is expensive when purchased in the small, refined cakes found in art and craft stores. If you are going to be using large quantities, I suggest you buy unrefined wax from an apiary. Clean the unrefined wax of any impurities by melting it, and strain it through a double thickness of cheesecloth. Repeat the process two or three

nozzle. Look for gutta where you buy silk-painting supplies. Household laundry starch, watercolor masking fluid, and sugar-water syrup can also be used to create resist patterns.

DISCHARGE PASTE

Discharge paste is a bleaching agent that removes the color from areas of the fabric to which it is applied. You can use a solution of household bleach and water or purchase a commercial product from an art supply store or mail order company.

The strength of the bleach, the amount of time the bleach is left on the fabric, and the type, color and thickness of the fabric all play a part in determining the outcome of the discharge. A neutralizing finishing rinse of vinegar and water halts the bleaching action at the desired stage of color-removal.

FABRIC

Natural fabrics such as cotton, silk, linen, and rayon are the most compatible with the cold water batik dyes. There are dozens of natural fabrics to choose from and each one has its own unique characteristics that affect the application of both the wax and the dye. Color, thickness, nap, weave, texture, and finish all effect the final results. It is best to experiment with small swatches of a fabric before waxing and dyeing the final batik.

For obvious reasons, white fabric is most often used for batik. However fabric of solid colors and ones with printed designs can also provide interesting results. Colored fabrics are particularly striking when used for bold, two-color designs. Printed fabrics create interesting sub-patterns within a design.

The fabric's thickness effects the speed and the penetration of wax and the amount of dye needed. Very

Photo by Dan Snipes

heavy fabrics such as flannel or velvet are slow to absorb the wax thus they allow for a very slow application of the wax but must be waxed on both sides of the material to assure an even coverage. Medium

Angel, by Sandie McCann, 30"w x 48"h.

Indonesian batiks are overdyed, discharge dyed, and hand painted. Design is machine pieced, hand appliquéd, and hand embroidered. Machine embroidery by Kathleen Pappas.

weight fabrics such as cotton broadcloth, linen, Indian head, sheeting, and muslin also absorb the wax slowly but usually require application of the wax on only one side of the fabric. This makes them ideal for the novice crafter. Sheer fabrics such as silk and rayon absorb the wax very rapidly. The wax must be applied with speed and certainty to avoid any unwanted spread of the wax.

A thick-napped fabric's uneven absorption of wax leads to an uneven distribution of the dye. This can create interesting textural effects, subtle shadings, and ghost images in the final design. Sometimes the tip of the thick nap remains wax-free on the unwaxed side of the batik. When the fabric is dyed, this unwaxed area picks up the dye and appears in the finished design as colored fuzz over the resisted areas. Ghost patterns appear when the wax does not totally penetrate through the thick fabric, leaving minute fissures in the wax on the underside of the fabric. When the fabric is dyed these exposed areas pick up the dye and appear as subtle linear designs on the finished batik.

Fabric used for batik should be free of sizing, waterproofing, and other coatings that will interfere with the penetration of the dyes.

Fabrics ordered through batik supply companies are usually free of these added coatings but always check with the supplier to be sure. Most fabrics sold in fabric and craft stores are coated with starch and/or sizing and should be washed in warm, soapy water before they are used for batik. Experiment with a wide variety of fabrics. You will then be able to confidently select fabric to meet the unique requirements of each of your batik projects.

Dyeing Equipment

DYEBATH CONTAINERS

Select a non-reactive dyeing container that corresponds to the size of the fabric to be dyed. Small batiks fit into a shallow bowl or dish while larger ones can be dyed in a plastic wading pool, plastic storage bin, wallpaper trough, or laundry tub.

Whether you use a bucket, plastic wading pool, or a large storage bin, plan ahead for the method of emptying the container and rinsing the fabric. You might even want to fill the container with water, not dye, and practice emptying it before going ahead with the dyes. My very large batiks were dyed in my studio's bathtub. At first I tried lining the tub with a plastic drop cloth, but I eventually settled for the inevitable rings of color around the tub, which I periodically removed with scouring powder. I strung clothesline over the tub and hung the batiks up while I prepared the rinse water. The rinsed batiks were also hung over the tub to drip-dry.

CLOTHESLINE AND CLOTHESPINS

Use non-absorbent plastic clothes line and plastic clothespins. Wash and rinse them thoroughly after each use to prevent dye from contaminating the next batik. Woven

Leaf Studies
by Sandra Holley, Marie Dorr, Donna Hickman, Bernice Meissner, 27"w x 27"h.

Wax resist on thick-napped cotton flannel.

Photo by Edward Kessler

cotton rope and wooden pins absorb dye, which is then discharged onto the next piece of fabric even after they have been cleaned. A folding wooden rack can be used in place of a clothesline. Cover the rungs with plastic wrap to prevent the wood from absorbing the dye and staining the next batik.

Storage Containers

Some dyes can be saved and reused. Store them in clean containers and kept in a cool, dark place. Quart canning jars or gallon milk cartons make convenient storage vessels. Keep in mind that the pigment strength of used dye may be greatly reduced even if the color looks deep and strong.

Dyeing Tools

Measuring Cup and Spoons

Keep non-reactive measuring spoons, stirrer, and measuring cups with your batik supplies and do not use them for food preparation. Avoid using metal equipment other than stainless steel, for it can react unfavorably with the chemicals in the dyes.

Strainer and Cheesecloth

An extra-fine non-reactive mesh strainer lined with a double thickness of cheesecloth filters out undissolved particles of dye. This is a critical step in preparation of acid dyes, which can be difficult to dissolve.

Dyeing Materials

Dyes

The type of fabric to be dyed, the resist substance used, the desired color, and personal preference all play a part in the selection of dye from the wide assortment that is available. The two most popular chemical dyes used for batik are acid dyes and fiber-reactive dyes. Information on dyes and dyeing techniques is presented in Chapter 5.

Mordants

The mordant is a chemical or mineral additive that makes the dye permanent. Each dye product has its own required mordant and special process for using it. Acid dyes are made permanent on cotton with a mordant of salt. Acid dyes on silk require household vinegar. Fiber-reactive dyes use an alkali to trigger the molecular bonding of the color and fiber.

Urea

Urea is an ammonia compound that acts as a wetting agent. It is recommended for use with fiber-reactive dyes because it helps to dissolve the dye granules and also keeps the fabric moist while the color reacts with the fabric.

Calgon

Calgon is a brand name of water softener. It is added to fiber-reactive dye to neutralize any harmful mineral content in the water.

Calsolene Oil

This is a wetting agent recommended for immersion dyeing with fiber-reactive dyes. It is used to break the surface tension of the water, allowing the dye to penetrate the fibers more easily.

Salt

Table salt, Resist Salt L, or Glauber's Salt is added to the dye to enhance the color. It can also be sprinkled onto the wet, dyed fabric to create interesting textural effects.

Activator

Fiber-reactive dyes require the addition of an alkali to trigger the molecular process between color and fiber. Soda ash and bicarbonate of soda (baking soda) are two common activators. Activator is sometimes referred to as a "fixer".

Synthropol

Synthropol is a detergent that removes oil and sizing from the fabric. It also keeps the particles of dye suspended in the water, preventing them from staining the fabric.

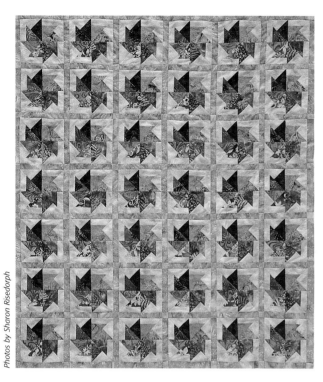

Pinwheels (and detail) by Cathy Miranker, 65"w x 78"h.

Machine pieced from a variety of commercial batik fabrics.

SODIUM ALGINATE

This is a seaweed product that is used to thicken the dyes.

WATERPROOF GLOVES

Protect your hands by wearing waterproof gloves every time you handle the dyes. Heavy work gloves are sturdy, inexpensive, and available in grocery stores. While they last through repeated uses, the thickness of the latex makes for an awkward fit and prevents you from feeling the correct temperature of the dyebath. Lab gloves made of latex or vinyl are sold in boxes of 100 at most drugstores and medical supply centers. They fit snugly, permit you to feel hot and cold, but are less durable.

FACE MASK

A facemask prevents the inhalation of airborne particles of dye and should be worn whenever you are handling powdered dyes and other chemicals. Hardware stores, medical supply shops and drugstores all carry a variety of masks. A special respirator mask should be used to filter out noxious fumes.

Wax Removal Supplies

IRON

A household iron is used to melt the wax from the fabric. Use a non-steam setting at the temperature appropriate for the type of fabric you are ironing. The iron will get a bit waxy, particularly inside the steam jets, so I recommend that you set aside an iron just for your batik work. If you must use the iron to press clothing, clean it thoroughly and flush it out with distilled water.

NEWSPAPERS

It takes a lot of newspaper to absorb the wax during the ironing process. Pad the ironing surface with a thick pile and cover the top sheet with unprinted newsprint to prevent the ink from staining the fabric.

UNPRINTED NEWSPRINT

A sandwich of unprinted paper will absorb the wax and protect the fabric from newspaper ink during the ironing process. Newspaper publishers often give away, or sell at minimal cost, the ends of bolts left from the printing process. Check with your local newspapers. Large pads of unprinted newsprint can be purchased at an art supply store or a school-supply shop but are considerably more expensive.

SOLVENTS

I find it hard to believe that in the early days of my batik explorations I would blithely fill a basin with Energene and slosh the waxy fabric in it to remove the wax. This was done without benefit of gloves and mask so not only did it fail to thoroughly remove the wax, but it also filled the room, and my lungs, with dangerous fumes, and coated my hands with hazardous, skin-absorbing chemicals. Luckily I survived to tell the tale, but l do not recommend the use of solvents for the removal of wax. They are flammable and are very caustic to sensitive mucus membranes when inhaled. They also can cause irreparable damage when absorbed through the skin. If there is a trace of wax left in the batik that must be removed, take the piece to a reputable dry-cleaning shop.

Photos by Chris Eden

Sunday Morning: Oak Bluffs, Martha's Vineyard
by Susan Schneider,
25"w x 34"h.

from the edge of the table. To be safe, keep a fire extinguisher within reach of your workstation. Store chemicals in tight-lid jars and keep them away from children, pets, and foodstuffs.

Cover the table top with a piece of fabric or heavy paper. Place the batik frame on the table-cover in the position that you would set a dinner plate. Set the electric frying pan nearest the hand you will use to hold the tools. I am right-handed so I situate the pan at the upper right-hand corner of the frame in easy reach as I sit at the table. Also keep a container of pushpins and thumbtacks, a pencil, ruler, and the tjantings and brushes near at hand.

On the opposite side of the frame keep the assortment of lesser-used tools and folded paper towel to hold under the tjanting's spout as you move the tool from the frying pan to the fabric. Convenient, though not necessary, is a bulletin board on which to tack up your design ideas, color swatches, and inspirations.

In Summary

You now have all the supplies you need and are ready to try your hand at batik. Turn to the next chapter for information on applying the wax to fabric and let the fun begin!

The Workstation

The work area needn't be large or fancy. A table near an electrical outlet, a chair, one bin or box to hold the waxing supplies and one to hold the dyeing supplies, and a place to keep all the supplies out of harm's way when you are not using them are all you need. Minimal waxing supplies include an electric frying pan, paraffin, a small frame, thumbtacks or pushpins, fabric, brushes and tjantings, and paper towels.

Dyeing supplies include cold-water batik dyes, color-setting mordants, strainer and cheesecloth, measuring spoons and cup, bowl, clothesline, and clothespins. You will also need a stash of old newspapers, some unprinted newsprint, and an iron.

However simple the workstation, make safety the prime consideration in its arrangement. Maintain the electrical equipment, place electrical cords out of the room's traffic pattern, and position the container of melted wax away

3

Waxing Methods

Tradition, innovation, and improvisation all have a role in the process of applying wax to fabric. This crucial step creates the areas of the design that are to remain totally free of dye and also is used to retain the desired color at each step in a multiple-colored design. Originally, batik was probably created with a cold paste resist that was brushed, squeezed, dabbed, or dropped onto the fabric. A cone, much like a pastry bag, was often used to extrude the paste in fine, controlled lines and dots. Sometimes the paste was applied to the entire surface of the fabric and then raked with a comb-like tool to create linear designs. As hot wax became the favored resist medium, brushes, tjantings, and stamps were developed as the most common tools for applying the wax to fabric.

The selection of the tool determines the placement and control of the wax, thus the look of the final design. Minute wax dots applied with a tjanting create delicate and controlled patterns while quick, bold brush strokes of wax create powerful, sweeping motifs. The application tool selected, the wax formula, the thickness of the resist, and the manipulations of the waxed areas all effect the final outcome of the waxing.

Photo by artist

Surge, by Ginny Lohr, 40"w x 30"h.

Bold brushstrokes of resist and dye were hand painted onto Thai silk. Then the fabric was ironed to partially remove the wax before sections of the batik were over-dyed with yellow and purple.

Brushes

There are thousands of different brushes, each with unique characteristics that effect the markings that it produces. The outcome of brush-applied resist reflects the type, firmness, and absorbency of bristles and bristle configuration — shape, width, length, volume.

One or two natural-bristled brushes are all you need to begin applying the wax to fabric. A Japanese watercolor or calligraphy brush with boar bristles secured to a bamboo handle is a good choice for beginners. The round shape tapers to a fine point that can be used to create lines and shapes of all sizes and intricacies. Also useful is a broad, blunt-ended brush for creating stripes, bands, and large solid areas. As you become skilled in using these brushes you will probably want to add a variety of others to your cache of waxing tools.

Experiment on some practice fabric before tackling a final design. Set up your workstation, melt the wax and stretch a piece of fabric on the frame. Keep a folded paper towel near at hand and use it to catch drips as you move the brush from the pan

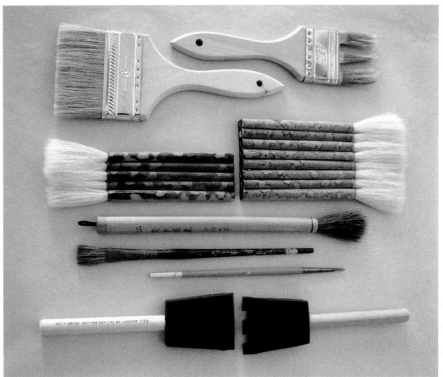

to the fabric. I suggest that you do not try to create a specific design at first, but rather, just enjoy getting the feel of applying the wax with a brush.

Grip the brush as you would a pencil and dip the bristles into the melted wax. Hold the brush there for a few moments to heat the bristles, then quickly move it to the fabric and glide it across the surface. The wax will cool immediately and appear as a shiny, translucent sealant. Return the brush to the wax to reheat, and check the underside of the cloth to make sure the wax

Photo by Bernice Meissner

APPLYING WAX WITH BRUSHES

1 Applying wax with a bamboo brush .

2 Applying wax with a sable brush.

3 Applying wax with a notched sponge brush.

Photos by Nicolas Kane

has completely penetrated the fibers. If the wax appears as an opaque film on top of the surface or has not soaked completely through the fabric, increase the temperature of the wax before continuing the waxing process.

If you use an electric frying pan to heat the wax you probably find that the brushes do not stay propped at the side of the pan. Embed a thumbtack partway into the end of each brush's wooden handle. This serves to hook the brushes to the side of the pan, preventing them from sinking into the wax.

APPLYING BRUSH LINES

Lines are the most basic marks of a brush. They reproduce with exactitude the hand's motion and energy. Swift, sure strokes and bold flourishes leave distinctively different marks from smooth, steady gestures, or light, delicate ones. Practice applying lines in a variety of ways. Use each of your brushes to apply broad, sweeping marks and slow, deliberate ones. Draw lines that barely skim the surface of the fabric and create others by firmly pressing the brush into the cloth. Alternate the pressure of the brush as you wax a single line and observe the difference the pressure makes on the width of the line. Be inventive. These marks do not have to look like anything in particular — they are just for your own delight and discovery.

Practice will also stimulate your creativity and you will find that innovative design ideas will spring from your newfound skills.

POSITIVE LINES are formed by waxing all the areas surrounding the line. The unwaxed line will accept the dye and appear in the finished batik as a solid, dark area on a light background. Use a narrow brush if the space around the positive line is narrow and a broad one if the area is large.

Right: *Mourning Klee* by Chuck Kaiser, 13"w x 21"h.

Bold, positive brush lines.

Below: Jess in Hat by Jessica Hughes, 20"w x 14"h

Energetic negative brush lines.

Photo by Annmarie Kaiser

Photo by artist

Photo by artist

Temple of Castor and Pollux
by Bernadette DiPietro, 21"w x 27"h.

Painting on paper was sealed with
hot wax. Cracks were then created
before the piece was overdyed.

tail of brush marks at the end of the line.

DELICATE LINES are carefully applied with a narrow detail brush. Take special care to see that very fine marks soak through the fabric. Lines that have not totally penetrated the fabric can be rewaxed from the back of the cloth, but this will often thicken the line, thus changing the original look of the design.

PARALLEL LINES can be evenly waxed by using a notched brush. Cut away sections of a wide varnishing brush to form the desired pattern. Apply even pressure as you apply the wax to keep all the parallel lines an even width.

Applying Solid Areas

A brush makes quick work of sealing solid areas of a design. Apply a thin even coating of bees-wax-rich resist to avoid unwanted veining. Use straight paraffin to create cracks and crazing.

LARGE AREAS of solid color can be sealed quickly and easily with a broad, flat tipped varnish or trim brush. Overlap the brushstrokes to avoid unwanted ghost lines.

INTRICATE AREAS are best waxed with the point of a calligraphy brush or a fine detail brush. Make sure the wax is hot enough to penetrate the entire thickness of fabric in the first application.

CRACKS AND CRAZING are often a part of batik designs. Solid coatings of pure paraffin can be scrunched, folded, pleated, and pinched to create random and controlled patterns.

NEGATIVE LINES are waxed directly onto the cloth. When the fabric is dyed the lines will remain the color of the cloth at the time of their waxing. Because negative lines are applied in a direct manner, they are most likely to retain the energy of their application.

GHOST LINES are hair-thin lines that appear when the brushstrokes of wax meet but do not overlap. Tiny fissures of open fabric between the strokes accept the dye and appear as fine, linear patterns.

SWEEPING LINES denote the motion of the brush and the pattern of the bristles. Use a stiff brush to swiftly and firmly apply the wax. Draw the line and lift the brush off the fabric in a single, smooth motion to leave a wispy

RESEALING AREAS prevents unwanted cracks and crazing in the finished design. Wax, particularly paraffin, erodes when the fabric is repeatedly dyed, rinsed and re-stretched. If the wax begins to lift off the fabric, rewax the worn areas with a broad brush. A small amount of bees wax added to the paraffin will keep the wax more pliable and less likely to erode.

At first you may feel a bit awkward applying the wax with a brush, but keep at it. Your skills will develop and eventually you will be able to wax the most challenging of motifs. Don't worry about making mistakes. Even the most practiced batik artist will occasionally spill drops of wax onto the fabric. Most of the time these small drips can be ignored for they will not interfere with the pattern. If an unplanned area of wax is particularly bothersome you can incorporate it into the design by making a few minor changes to the motif. As a last resort, remove all the wax from the fabric and rewax the completed areas of the design before applying the next dyebath.

Tjantings

The tjanting is the most traditional tool used to apply wax to fabric. The smooth, linear stream of wax bonding with the fabric as it flows from the tjanting is a kinesthetic pleasure that many batik artists find immensely satisfying and inspirational.

The rapidity of the wax flow and the brief intervals of work time between refills are challenges for even the most experienced artisan. To get a feel for the tjanting it is best to practice before undertaking a specific project. Arrange your work surface and heat the wax.

Hold the tjanting by its wooden handle much like you would a pencil. For safety's sake never touch the metal reservoir or the melted wax. Dip the bowl of the tjanting into the melted wax and hold it there for a few seconds to heat before filling the reservoir with the hot wax. Make a

APPLYING WAX WITH TJANTING

1 Applying wax with a tjanting.

2 Applying wax with an Indonesian tjanting.

3 Applying wax with a tjanting on cotton.

4 Applying wax with tjanting on silk.

Photos by Nicolas Kane

drip-catcher from a small pad of absorbent fabric or paper and hold it under the spout as you move the tool from the wax to the fabric. You are now ready to apply the wax.

Glide the tjanting over the fabric, barely skimming the surface. The hot wax will quickly penetrate the entire thickness of the cloth and instantly cool and harden, leaving a shiny, translucent coating that can be seen on both sides of the fabric. When dyed sections of fabric are waxed, the wax darkens and masks the actual color of the fabric. The true color will not appear again until the wax is removed. This element of surprise and revelation is part of the intrigue of the craft.

If the wax does not flow through the spout with ease, or cools before soaking into the fabric and appears as a white film on the top surface of the fabric, increase the temperature of the wax. If the wax is too runny, let the wax-filled tjanting cool for a few seconds before applying the wax to the fabric.

APPLYING TJANTING LINES

Lines are a natural extension of the tjanting. Smooth and seamless, they pour from the spout to form fluid, organic ribbons, intricate geometric patterns and bold outlines, stripes and grids. They have been used as dominant design elements throughout the long and culturally diverse history of batik. Lines are sometimes used as the single element of a design but more often they are combined with shapes, textures and dots to form complex motifs.

Practice making a variety of lines with each of the three sizes of tjantings. Keep the tjanting moving across the fabric at all times. Resting it on one spot, even for a moment, will create a blob along the otherwise smooth line.

The speed of the motion and the size of the spout effect the thickness

Above: *Sarah* (front & back) by Shelley Thornton, 25" tall.

Batik spirals embellish the fabric used to create the unique cloth-constructed hairdo.

Right: *Using an electric tjanting.*

of the line. The faster the tjanting is drawn across the fabric, the narrower the line of wax will be. Also, the narrower the spout, the narrower the line. If the wax flows too freely from even the narrowest of spouts, try placing a miniscule amount of fabric lint into the reservoir. This will partially block the spout, slowing the flow of the wax. If all else fails, use a pair of pliers to partially close the end of the spout. Keep practicing and you will soon be creating lines of all widths and lengths and incorporating them into your batik motifs.

POSITIVE LINES are created by waxing the area surrounding the line. When the unwaxed area is dyed it stands out as a dark line on a light background.

Photos by artist

Photo by Dave Lenox, courtesy of Natalie Guess

NEGATIVE LINES are those that are waxed directly onto the fabric. When the batik is completed these lines will appear as light lines on the darker fabric.

NET DESIGNS are surface motifs that fill a specific area with a taut network of lines. These lines whether positive, negative, or a combination of both, can vary in thickness or be uniformly even. They connect to various points along the border of the fabric, creating a tension that holds the design in place across the surface. One color net designs are a good exercise for practicing with the tjanting.

OUTLINING creates a strong, smooth border around a design element. This border can be used to define a positive shape or it can be filled in with solid wax to create a negative space.

WALLING-IN refers to the method of totally inclosing a section of a design with a solid line of wax. Dye is then brushed onto the enclosed shape. The wall of wax acts as a barrier, preventing the color from spreading into other sections of the design. Dyeing techniques and color combinations not possible with the overlapping colors of immersion dyeing are feasible with this technique.

Photo by artist

Left: *Diagonals*, by Kay Baxandall, 26"w x 19.5"h.

Net design with negative and positive lines.

Below Left: *Our Gang*, by Muffy Clark Gill, 40"w x 30"h.

Negative and positive lines.

Below Right: *Shaman*, by Gretchen Lima, 25" tall.

Mixed media doll with batik fabrics.

Photo by Ed Chappell

Photo by Bill Lemka

GHOST LINES are fine, hair-thin lines that appear when a solid area is filled in with tjanting lines that touch but do not overlap. Barely perceivable fissures between the lines of wax will fill with dye to create faint linear patterns.

TEXTURAL AREAS add visual interest to a design. The tjanting can be used to fill in sections of the design with straight lines, swirls, and cross-hatching.

APPLYING SOLID AREAS

Solid areas of the design are easily filled in with the tjanting. The smallest size tool is best for intricate shapes while the bigger tools make quick work of large areas. Areas of solid wax can be pinched, creased, and cracked to form the veining that is often a part of batik.

NARROWING THE TJANTING SPOUT

Apply pressure slowly and evenly with pliers to avoid damaging the delicate spout.

Below: *Ladies Afternoon Out*, by Terri Haugen, 40"w x 30"h.
Foreground shapes contrast with the busy background texture.

Left:
Sand Dunes
by Eloise Piper,
50"w x 68"h.

Dots of wax
and color
shading create
the dimensional
effect of the
dunes.

Below:
*Childhood
Meadow*
(detail)
by Eloise Piper.

Layers of
overlapping
dots form
the treetops.

Photo by William Zinner

Photo by Edward Kessler

APPLYING DOTS

Designs that utilize dots represent the epitome of skill and control that batik artists aspire to master. Distinctively textured shapes and lines consisting of hundreds of small dots created with the tjanting are found in many traditional motifs, particularly those from Java. Contemporary batik artists use dots in the traditional manner and also to create gradations of color and innovative textures and shadings.

Delicately dotted lines and lacy shapes not only provide interesting contrasts to solid lines and shapes, but the dots of wax also have the advantage of being flexible and less prone to cracking because of the small amount of surface that each individual dot covers.

Drops of wax, some no larger than the head of a pin, are carefully applied with the narrowest of the tjantings. Adjust the wax to the desired temperature and fill the tjanting's reservoir. Lightly touch the surface of the fabric. Immediately lift the tjanting off the surface. Repeat this procedure, carefully placing each dot within the desired motif.

The temperature of the wax is critical to this procedure. If the wax is not hot enough, the dot will cool before soaking into the fabric and appear as an opaque white bead on the surface. If the wax is too hot, it will pour from the spout in an uncontrolled manner or spread into a large spot rather than a tiny dot.

POINTILLISM, first developed by the French Impressionists, is a method of painting with dots of color, which the eye then blends to form new hues and shadings. This method can be successfully applied to batik. For instance a blend of yellow and red dots will appear as orange while yellow and dark green blend to a bright, light green. Understanding color, particularly the combining of different hues, is important when incorporating pointillism in your batik designs.

OVERLAPPING DOTS create a complex textural pattern. Wax and dye a pattern of dots. When the final layer of dye is dry, remove the wax and apply a fresh layer of dots in an offset pattern over the first layer. Dye the fabric with a contrasting hue. The resulting pattern provides a depth not usually achieved with batik methods.

SHADING is achieved through the pointillist use of dots and the subtle application of dyes ranging from light to dark. Apply a pattern of dots at one side of a designated shape and dye the fabric the lightest of colors. Apply more dots alongside and overlapping the first dots and dye the design the next darker color. Repeat dotting the wax and dyeing the fabric in progressively darker shades as you gradually work around to the opposite side of the shape.

POSITIVE DOTS, those that appear as dark marks on the light fabric, are created by waxing the area surrounding the dots. The fabric is then dyed and the small areas of unwaxed fabric appear as dark dots on a light background.

NEGATIVE DOTS appear as light spots on a darker area. They are waxed directly onto the desired layer of color.

Techniques using the tjanting are as varied as the many artists who express themselves in the medium of batik. It is as if the flow of wax primes a stream of visual ideas, experiments, and images that pour forth effortlessly from their fertile imaginations. Each artist develops special nuances — a special grip of the handle, a turn or lift of the spout, a thoughtful matching of wax flow to fabric selection. These subtleties are often so familiar that they seem to

be an intuitive extension of the hand; a link to the mind's eye. No matter your initial experience with the tjanting, practice, patience, and a special love of the batik process are all that you need to develop your skills. Soon the tjanting will become the means for your unique and personal expression.

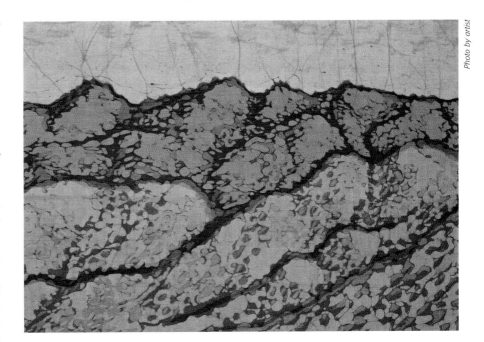

Photo by artist

Photo by artist

Above Top: *Desert Mountains*
by Stephanie Love,
24"w x 18"h.

Above Bottom:
Staithes, Afternoon
by Heather Gatt, 48cm x 36cm.

Dots, daubs and solid areas
create glistening water.

Photo by Dave Lenox, courtesy of Natalie Guess

Photo by Nicolas Kane

Assorted commercial fabrics, courtesy of Princess Mirah Designs, Bali Fabrics.

Cotton embellished with tjap applied wax, hand painted dyes, discharge dyeing.

Stamps

Stamping tools called *tjaps* have been used for centuries to apply wax designs to fabric. Developed as a short cut to the laborious method of hand waxing, these stamps made possible a thriving export business of batik fabrics in both Malaysia and Europe. Originally the tjap consisted of a linear relief pattern carved into a wooden block. The relief pattern was imbedded with bands of narrow copper and a handle was attached to the back of the block. Today the tjap is likely to be made entirely of metal. Some tjaps are constructed of two mirror-image stamps, which are carefully aligned to stamp the wax on both sides of the fabric.

The wax design is printed onto the fabric in the same manner as an inked design of a wood block. The block is dipped into hot wax to heat the metal and coat it with the wax, and the block is then pressed onto the fabric, discharging the wax into the fabric. This process is repeated, carefully registering the design to create a seamless repeat of the pattern.

While stamping was originally developed to hasten the laborious waxing process, today it is also used to add a distinctive new dimension to the batik process. Stamped design motifs are no longer limited to those created from the intricately carved tjaps. Markings can be as varied as the numerous objects used create them.

You can create original stamps from ordinary household objects. Make stamps by embedding designs of round-headed nails into blocks of wood or large corks. Cut interesting shapes from heavy cardboard and regular household sponges and glue a spool or a bead to the back of each shape to serve as a handle. Lines can be stamped with the edges of heavy cardboard. Cut the cardboard into different lengths or bend it into interesting configurations. Common items such as corks, cookie cutters, cores from rolls of toilet paper, and the flat ends of bamboo brushes can also serve as stamps. I like to use paper for these early experiments because even the most experimental of patterns can be used for interesting wrapping paper or for a variety of craft projects.

Hold the stamp by its handle or from the back, keeping your fingers away from the hot wax. Dip the stamp into the wax and hold it there for a second or two. Quickly move the stamp to the fabric or paper and press it onto the surface. Carefully lift it straight up from the surface to avoid unwanted smears or smudges and return the stamp to the wax.

Check the back of the fabric or paper to make sure the wax has penetrated the entire thickness. Repeat the procedure with a variety of stamping items and observe the difference in line quality and absorbency.

STRIPES are created by arranging the design elements in rows. Freehand placement creates stripes with a spontaneous look while guidelines of masking tape aid in creating precise, evenly placed stripes.

BORDERS add a distinctive touch to clothing and accessories. They can also be used to create a finishing edge on pictorial batiks.

ALL-OVER PATTERNS can be randomly stamped over the entire surface or carefully placed within a network of grid lines. Avoid unwanted pencil marks on the batik by using masking tape to create these guidelines.

REGISTERED DESIGNS appear as precise, seamless motifs. Carefully align each imprint to create equal distance between the repeated elements of the design.

The spontaneous nature of the stamping process encourages improvisation and experimentation.

STAMPING

Stamping with cork.

Stormy Peaks, by Susan Stein, 42"w x 43"h.
Commercial tjap-stamped batiks and hand dyed clothespin-resist fabrics. Machine pieced and quilted. Embellished with hand sewn bugle beads.

INCISING A WAXED BATIK

Photo by Bernice Meissner

Photo by Randy Cullen

Dancing with Butterflies
by Lila Hahn,
29"w x 25"h.

Here is a chance to explore your creative response to the medium without a lot of rules of right or wrong. The use of inexpensive papers rather than fabrics also allows a more impromptu response to the craft and provides original wrapping paper as well. So have fun and don't worry about the results. Sometimes it's the process, not the product, that is the most important focus of artistic expression.

Incising Tools

Delicate, hand-drawn patterns are created by carving lines into solid areas of wax to expose the fabric beneath. When the fabric is dyed, these exposed areas absorb small amounts of color and appear as faint lines in the finished design. It takes no special tool to carve linear patterns into the wax. You can use a knitting needle, ice pick, small nail, blunt yarn-darner, or just about any sharp-ended stylus. I prefer to use a round-tipped dental tool.

Brush an even covering of wax over the desired area of fabric. Use a mixture of paraffin and bees wax to assure that the coating will not crack when manipulated. Using a stylus, scratch lightly into the wax and lift off the shaving of wax. Repeat, gradually working down to uncover the surface of the fabric. Be careful not to snag or cut the fabric as you scratch the wax away.

Submerge the fabric in the dye, gently rubbing the color into the exposed groves. Because the fabric was saturated with wax *before* the lines were incised, the carved pattern will not absorb the full strength of the dye and therefore will appear less intense in color than unwaxed areas of fabric.

SINGLE-COLORED LINES are created when all the incised lines are sealed with wax after they are dyed one specific color. Light, subtle lines appear when the lines are filled after one or two dyebaths. Dark, high-contrast lines appear when the grooves are left open until the final dyebath is applied.

MULTIPLE-COLORED LINES within the same design are created by carefully sealing only portions of the incised design after each dyeing. Subtle changes in line color can create a look of depth and volume.

In Summary

There is no one *correct* way to apply wax resist. It can be drawn, stamped, or carved with many different tools using a variety of techniques. Each brush, tjanting, stamp, and incising tool has unique characteristics that effect the way in which the wax is applied and every batik artist has special techniques that add individual nuances to the procedure.

No matter how they apply the wax, batik artists derive immense satisfaction from the process. They are excited and inspired by the fluid glide of the wax, the bonding of image to fiber, and the anticipation of the final revelation of color after the wax has been removed. Most will tell you they have an intuitive *feel* for the waxing process, a sixth sense that is hard to explain or teach to others. Their hands and eyes just seem to know what to do. In reality, this sixth sense is not a magical occurrence but rather a love of the creative process, a logical understanding of the medium, and a kinesthetic and sensory response to the craft based on experience.

If you have never created designs with hot wax, you may find that your first efforts seem awkward and the results crude, but persevere. With each attempt your skills will increase and your confidence grow. In time, with a little patience and practice, you too will develop that intuitive response to the waxing process that comes from knowledge and experience. You will also gain immense satisfaction from the evolution of your creativity.

The Fire Within
by Vikki Pignatelli,
64"w x 62"h.

Photo by Robert Groh

4

Using Color

Color saturates our world. It stirs our senses, stimulates our emotions, and excites our imagination. It affects us directly — no interpretation, explanation, or cognitive filter needed. People from all times and all places have been fascinated with color and have used it to beautify themselves and their surroundings. Color is also used to define and symbolize religious and cultural mores, social structures, and standards of beauty.

Color is one of the basic elements of visual art. It is used to give form, emotional content, and meaning to a work of art. No matter the media or the subject matter, a work of art's success depends largely on the selection and arrangement of color. In order to use color effectively it is important to know something about the nature of color and the basics of color nomenclature.

The Additive System

There are two different systems by which to understand color: The study of light, or the additive system, and the study of pigment, the subtractive system. The additive system applies to color that comes from light. A light ray is made up of wavelengths that vibrate at varying speeds. Our eyes and brain are stimulated by these waves and interpret

Photo by artist

Hidden Passion
by Susan Stein,
51"w x 62"h.

Jonquils, by Arnelle Dow, 16"w x 20"h.

Photo by artist

each length as a different color. When you refract, or bend, a beam of light you can see these distinctively different colored waves of red, orange, yellow, green, blue, and violet. This band of colors is called the spectrum. A wide variety of colors are created through combining different wavelengths. When all the wavelengths are combined, or added together, they produce white light.

Color that comes from light rays is the purest and brightest form of color.

The Subtractive System

The beauty and purity of light inspires artist and artisan alike. We resonate to the works of the Impressionist painters largely because of

their exuberant use of light-defining color. For them, to see and capture the essence of pure light with pigment was to capture the essence of the moment. Their glowing scenes of everyday life seem to come alive because of the glorious, light-drenched palette of colors. But no matter how bright their paints, the artists could only approximate the colors that they were trying to

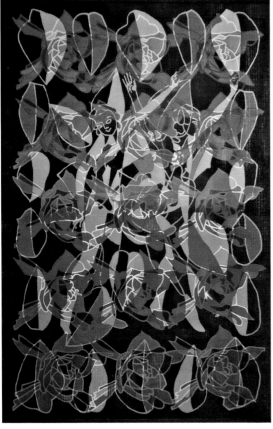

La Spectre de la Rose I
by Sheila Cook,
17"w x 27"h.

capture. This is because of the nature of the pigment that is used to represent light's colors.

The use of pigment is based on the subtractive system. Every colored object has pigmentation that absorbs, or subtracts, certain wavelengths while reflecting others. This absorption allows us to perceive the remaining, reflected color. A leaf absorbs all the wavelengths but green, the petals of a sunflower all but yellow. The artists' colors, whether oil paints, acrylics, pastels, or dyes, are substances that contain pigments that absorb and reflect. When these substances are applied to a surface, they impart their color characteristics to that surface. Even though pigment colors are similar to the colors that come from light,

the reflected light is not as pure as refracted light. Most surfaces reflect more than one color. This reduces the intensity of the color so that it only approximates the purity of light's color. The remaining discussion on color focuses on the pigment colors used by artists rather than the colors derived from light.

The Color Wheel

To successfully use color in a work of art it is necessary to understand the relationship between the various colors and to know how to mix pigments.

There are a variety of color systems that identify colors and demonstrate their relationships.

Sir Isaac Newton, Johann Wolfgang von Goethe, Arthur Schopenhauer, Wilhelm Ostwald, and Josef Albers are just a few of the color theorists of past centuries. Since the 1940s The United States Bureau of Standards has used Albert Munsell's system to name colors. The Munsell system assigns every color an identifying name and number and places it in a specific location on a circular, three-dimensional grid.

Of all the color systems, the color wheel is the simplest and the easiest to use. A basic color wheel includes the three primary colors and three secondary colors. Others include six or more intermediate colors. More complex wheels display numerous gradations of each color.

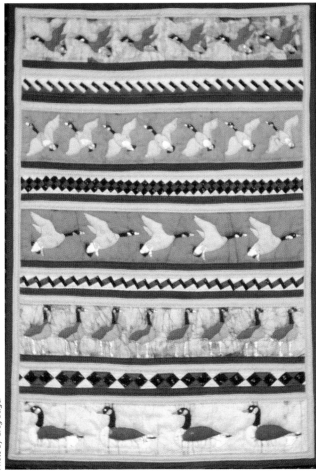

Photo by Greg Seigel

Left: *Geese Quilt*
by Rebekka Seigel,
36"w x 55"h.

Primary colors.

Below: *He Restoreth My Soul*
by Marilyn Salomon,
24"w x 20"h.

Secondary colors.

Photo by artist

PRIMARY COLORS of red, yellow and blue are spaced equal distances from each other on the color wheel. They are called primary because they are the first colors — the ones from which all other color is derived. Primary colors originate from specific pigments and cannot be mixed from other colors.

SECONDARY COLORS of green, orange, and violet are each created from a mixture of two primary colors. The secondary colors are also equal distance on the wheel and each is situated between the two primaries that produce it.

INTERMEDIATE COLORS such as red-orange, yellow-green, and blue-violet are derived from a mixture of a primary and a secondary color. Each of these colors lie in between the primary and secondary colors that create it.

THE SPECTRUM is the band of colors found in a beam of light. The spectrum colors include red, orange, yellow, green, blue, and violet. These plus white and black are used to create all the many thousands of colors that the human eye distinguishes.

Color Properties

Every color has three physical properties, or characteristics, that define it: hue, value and intensity.

HUE is another word for color. Hues are sometimes named to identify their location on the color wheel. Red, orange, and blue-violet are three of the hues on a color wheel. Sometimes hues are also given the names of objects that best describe them such as sky blue, barn red, and avocado green. Others such as yellow ochre and indigo blue are named for the substances that were originally used to create them.

Photo by artist

Left: *Seaside*
by Terri Haugen,
20"w x 30"h.

Low contrasting
values.

Kuta Sunset
by Linda Kaun,
22"w x 18"h.

High contrasting
values.

If you plan to use the primary colors to mix all the other hues, you must begin with true red, yellow and blue dyes. Printers and graphic artists refer to these primary colors as cyan (blue), magenta (red), and yellow. The brand names for dyes in these colors may vary so check with the manufacturer if you are unsure which dyes are the true primary colors.

VALUE pertains to the lightness or darkness of a color. To see a color's value just look at a black and white photograph where all the colors of life are transformed into black, white, and gray. These various blacks, whites, and all the many grays are values, not colors. White added to a color creates a lightened, or low value color called a tint. When black is added, the darkened, high value color is called a shade.

When you mix colors using a transparent coloring matter such as batik dye, tints are created through the addition of water in varying amounts, rather than white paint. Shades are produced with the addition of black dye, but I recommend that you use it with particular care. Too much black tends to muddy the color, which in turn will cloud all the successive layers of color.

INTENSITY refers to the brightness or dullness of a hue. Pure colors, or fully saturated colors, are rich and bright. Low intensity colors are duller and more subtle. Intense colors seem to advance to the forefront of a design while low intensity colors appear to recede into the background.

The pigment strength of batik dyes varies greatly. The manufacturers' color-chart swatches depict each hue at its fullest saturation. Follow the suggested ratio of dye to water to produce these intense colors. To decrease the dye's inten-

Photo by artist

sity dilute it with water or mix it with another color. Keep in mind that when two hues are combined, the resulting color is always less intense than either of the original hues. This is important to remember when you overlap the colors of your batiks.

Simultaneous Contrast

The hue, value and intensity are not unchanging, inherent traits of each color. This is because we seldom experience a color as a single, isolated entity. Usually one color is seen amid a variety of other colors. These surrounding colors affect the way in which we perceive the characteristics of a given color. When two different colors appear side by side, the contrast intensifies the difference between them. This phenomenon, called Simultaneous Contrast, is a most important factor to consider when selecting the palette and planning the placement of colors.

Batik artists employ the phenomenon of simultaneous contrast to create the appearance of a greater number of colors than are actually used in a piece. This is useful when a large palette is desired but the overlapping of the traditional dyebaths darkens and dulls the fabric after just a few layers of color. Any given color can be made to appear lighter when placed amid dark colors and darker when situated on lighter hues. You can also alter the intensity of a color in the same manner. A color will appear more intense when surrounding color is dull and dull when the area around it is brighter.

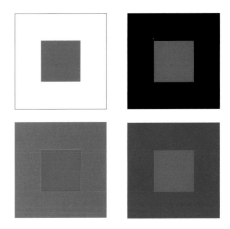

SIMULTANEOUS CONTRAST

Identical red squares on various background colors.

Confluences
by Jill Le Croissette,
36"w x 37"h.

Retaining Wall
by Eloise Piper, 26"w x 32"h.

Both upper and lower clouds of smoke are the identical color.

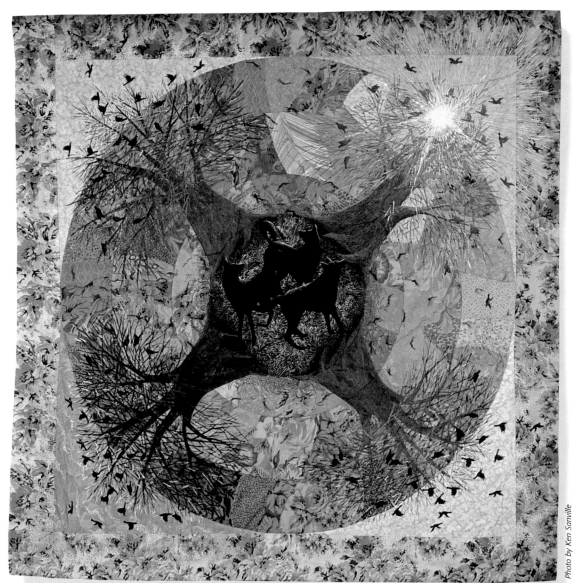

Left: *Blackbird Has Spoken* by Roxana Bartlett, 72"w x 72"h.

Cool-temperature colors dominate this haunting mixed media image.

Photo by Ken Sanville

Color Temperature

Every color has a visual temperature. Color temperature is used to organize the placement of color and to help define the emotional content. Red, yellow, and orange are warm colors and can be used to express passion, gaiety, anger, chaos and happiness. Cool colors of blue, green and violet can be used to represent sadness, chill, serenity, calm, and mystery. Colors of similar temperature create a look of harmo-ny while combinations of opposites create contrast.

A neutral-colored dye bath can be used as a transition between one color temperature and another. For example, when orange is overdyed with blue, the resulting color is usu-ally a brownish blue. If orange is first subdued with a dyebath of very pale blue, the resulting tan color is more easily changed to blue. Direct dyeing and walling-in dyes allow greater freedom in combining colors of varying temperatures.

Color Arrangements

There are a number of established color arrangements that aid in the successful use of color. Keep in mind that these are not static groupings of color but rather flexible guides that help organize and focus the work of art.

PRIMARY color arrangements of red, yellow and blue must be created from primary-colored pigments. This does not limit the variety of arrangements that can be created from these contrasting colors. For instance, navy, azure, pastel, periwinkle, ultramarine, teal, indigo, and cobalt are just a few of the many blue dyes available. Combine one of these with one each from the vast assortment of reds and yellows to create an unlimited variety of primary color schemes.

Walling-in and direct dyeing are the easiest methods of applying primary colors. The color scheme is more challenging when immersion dyebaths are used. Immersion dyeing requires a careful adjustment in both the amount of pigment used and the timing of each dyebath. Usually, yellow and red dyes overlap to produce orange and orange overlaps with blue creating brown. By reducing the intensity of the yellow dye, and overlapping it with a medium strength red dye, the overlapping color will remain red. A carefully timed dyebath of intense, dark blue over the red will result in a rich blue.

SECONDARY color arrangements of orange, green, and violet display a harmony that comes from their shared hues. Orange and green both contain the color yellow, green and violet contain the color blue, and violet and orange share the color red.

In batik, secondary color arrangements are easily achieved with immersion dyeing. This color combination can be created through the overlapping of primary colors or the use of secondary pigments or a combination of both. Orange is usually the lightest and thus the first color to apply. Whether pale or dark, bright or dull, orange can be overdyed with various shades of blue to create dull greens or dyed with green pigments for brighter shades. Saturated violet pigment will cover

Photo by William Zinner

Above: *Up and Away*
by Eloise Piper,
16"w x 22"h.

Overlapping dyebaths of the primary colors create a color scheme of yellow, orange and brown.

Right: *Songlines*
by Annie Phillips,
30"w x 36"h.

Primary color scheme.

Photo by Flash

Photo by Lynn Ruck

most green dyes while remaining strong and bright. Various changes in dye strength and dyebath timing of each color extend the possible combinations of secondary color arrangements.

MONOCHROMATIC colors are actually tints and shades of a single hue. Pink, scarlet, and maroon are all variations of the color red with the addition of white and black. This harmonic color scheme is one of the easiest to create with immersion dyeing. Start with a very diluted dyebath of the desired hue. Create a variety of tints by increasing the pigment strength with each successive dyebath. Add an increasing amount of black or mixtures of pigment plus black to create a variety of shades.

ANALOGOUS arrangements are made up of colors that share a common hue. These related colors are found side-by-side on the color wheel. For instance, the analogous colors of red, orange, and violet all contain the common color of red. This arrangement is well suited to the overlapping dyebaths of batik and the closely related colors provide unity within the complet-

Photo by artist

Right: *House Patterns*
by Eloise Piper,
40"w x 46"h.

Analogous color scheme.

Below: *Charleston Coastline*
(detail)
by Mary Edna Fraser.

Complementary color scheme.

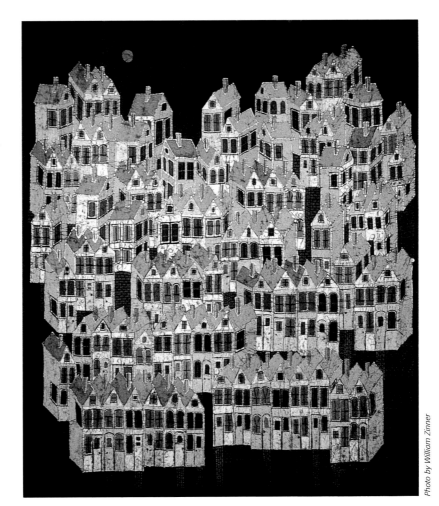

Photo by William Zinner

ed design. When using immersion dyebaths begin with the lightest color and gradually build to the darkest hue.

COMPLEMENTARY colors are any two hues that lie directly opposite one another on the color wheel. Whether you select the complements of red and green or yellow and violet or orange and blue, this arrangement displays the greatest amount of contrast because the colors are the furthest distance from each other on the wheel. When paired together, opposite colors contain, or complete, the three primary colors of yellow, red, and blue.

It is possible to create complementary color schemes with batik's immersion-dyeing process by varying the intensity of the two colors and adjusting the surrounding hues. Select the lightest and brightest color for the first dyebath. The dyebath of the opposite color will blend with the first color to create a darker and more subdued hue. This less intense color can be forced to appear brighter by surrounding it with duller, more neutral colors.

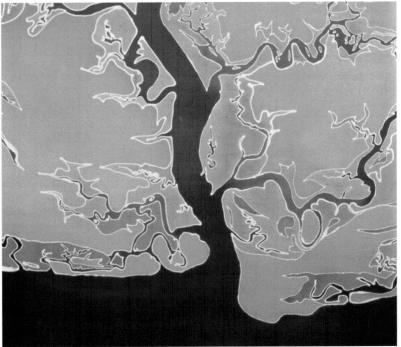

Photo by Terry Richardson

TRIAD arrangements consist of three equally spaced colors on the color wheel. The familiar primary and secondary color arrangements are two of the many triad possibilities. Select a triad color arrangement by placing an equilateral triangle on the color wheel. The points of the triangle will always align with three equal-distant colors.

TETRAD color schemes consist of four equally spaced colors. Place a square inside the color wheel and the corners will point to the contrasting quartet of colors.

POLYCHROMATIC color schemes utilize all the colors of the spectrum. It is a challenge to make a pleasing and organized arrangement from this unruly riot of colors. One solution is to use one color as the dominant hue and the other colors as subordinates and accents. This dominant color can define the foreground or the background.

This color scheme is one of the most difficult to create with the immersion dyeing process. It is far easier to create a polychromatic color arrangement with a combination of walling-in, direct dyeing, and immersion dyeing.

Photo by Bill Koplitz

Heron's Fisherman
by Katherine Hicks Tsonas,
48"w x 41"h.

Left: *Hello Mister*
by Linda Kaun,
40"w x 34"h.

Tetrad color scheme.

Below Left: *Crustacean Triptych III: Crab*
by Robin Paris,
22"w x 22"h.

Complementary color scheme.

Below Right: *Kaleidoscope Quilt* (detail)
by Nancy King,

Tetrad color scheme.

Photo by artist

Photo by artist

Photo by artist

Afternoon Stroll
by Lila Hahn,
33"w x 44"h.

Color Distribution

If all the selected colors of a particular arrangement were used in equal amounts, the effect would be chaotic and confusing even if the colors themselves were closely related. The eye would have a hard time finding a focus or a visual path to follow and the colors would all seem to be competing for attention rather than working together to make a pleasant concord. The careful proportioning of each color within a selected arrangement is the deciding factor in the creation of unity. I use an easy rule-of-thumb I call MOST, LESS, and LEAST to assure successful color distribution.

MOST represents the dominant color of the piece. It is the color that provides the over-all mood.

LESS designates the subordinate or secondary color. Used in a smaller amount than the dominant hue, the secondary color keeps the dominant color from becoming too monotonous. If this color is similar to the dominant color the result is one of close harmony. If it is an opposite, the result is contrast.

LEAST denotes the accent color, the one that often stands out the most even though it is used in the least amount. Sometimes the accent is in great contrast to the other two colors and sometimes it is within the same color family.

In Summary

You are now ready to experiment with actual pigments. Turn to chapter five for information on the various types of batik dyes, directions on mixing the dyes and coloring the fabric. No matter how much you understand about color on an intellectual basis, it is through hands-on trial and error that you really learn to create colors and combine them into successful arrangements.

Photo by artist

Above: *Small Town Provence*
by Ruth Holmes,

Triad color scheme.

Right: *Journeying to Freedom*
by Cherry Jackson,
250cm x 230cm.

African and Javanese batiks are
machine pieced and quilted.

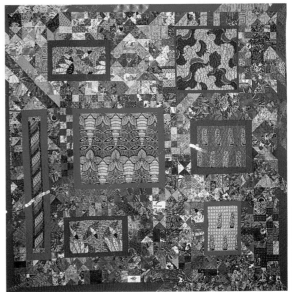

Photo by Tony Summers

5

Using Dyes

Batik is brought to life through the alchemy of the dye vat. The design may reflect imagination and the application of wax may display dexterity and skill, but it is the glorious color that unites the design, wax, and fabric into an integral whole. It is the dye that fuses the image with the very fibers of the batik, uniting process and product. It is the dye that transforms them into a work of art that transcends the mere sum of its parts.

Batik artists speak of that moment when the fabric meets color as being magical. All their planning, experience and labor come to fruition in an instant of combined intention and serendipity. The calculated and unexpected, the studied and capricious, suddenly meld and are made visible as the dye seeps into the fabric. The heart and soul of the work is revealed with the transforming, yet seemingly effortless, act of dipping fabric in dye.

The successful application of dye may seem effortless and intuitive, but in reality it develops from the artist's understanding of color, and a lot of hands-on experience with the various dyes and dyeing processes. Mastery of this information makes the dyeing process seem intuitive because it allows the artist to subordinate the process to personal vision.

Photo by Ned Pratt

Dawn, by Diana Dabinett, 40"w x 66"h.
Direct dyeing.

Categories of Dye

There are three main divisions of dye; natural dyes (animal, mineral, or vegetable based), aniline (coal tar-based), and chemical dyes (acid and fiber-reactive dyes to name a few). Each type of dye has its own unique formulas and physical properties, and its own palette of colors. While it is not necessary to know the molecular structure or the chemical formulas of each, it is helpful to have a rudimentary understanding of the source of various coloring agents, the role each has played in the development of batik, and some basics on how to mix and use them.

NATURAL DYES

Colors of the earth are the earliest known pigments — the ones first discovered by prehistoric peoples. Red clay iron-ore, cinnabar, and ochre were used to decorate masks, walls, and the human body. Thus began the search for more permanent and water-soluble dyestuffs that could be used to color fibers as well as artifacts and faces. Over the centuries colors were extracted from other mineral sources as well as various vegetable and animal matter. Roots, berries, bark, insects, even urine — all provided a source for early colorants.

In time, the juicy root of the wild herb madder was found to produce shades of red, and the leaves of the wild shrub woad yielded a blue pigment. The entire weld plant, sometimes called the *dyer's weed,* was used to create yellow, while wild broom added other shades of yellow to the palette of natural dyes. Buckhorn produced pink, and safflower red-violet. Versatile indigo provided a range of blues, violets, and black, and eventually took the place of woad as the dyers' preferred blue pigment. Indigo farms sprang up on every continent. In 1600 BC

Photo by artist

Above: *Char in Hammock*
by Jessica Hughes,
30"w x 24"h.

Direct dyeing.

Right: *Arches*
by Eloise Piper,
42"w x 52"h.

Immersion dyeing.

Photo by Edward Kessler

a purple coloring agent was discovered in the glandular secretion of a certain type of sea snail that grew along the shores of the eastern Mediterranean. Phoenician purple soon became the color of wealth and royalty throughout ancient Syria, Crete, Greece, and Rome. So precious was this color that under Nero's rule, death was the penalty for those who dared to wear it without authorization.

The Percian Phoenix
by dmotoko,
29"w x 19"h.

Immersion dyeing
with indigo dye
and silver leaf
embellishment.

Photo by Kazutaka Tamura

For centuries these and other colors extracted from animal, vegetable, and mineral substances were the mainstays of the dyeing industry. Unfortunately use of natural dyes claimed a heavy toll. Many dye-plants proved poisonous to the people who cultivated them, and the byproducts of dye production devastated the earth and water sources on which the dyeing industry depended. The lengthy, complicated dyeing procedures usually required a boiling process with the addition of various mordants to permanently set the natural dyes. These mordants also proved harmful to those who were forced to work with them. No wonder that in some countries workers in the dye business were held in bondage; forced by law to follow in their ancestors' trade.

The foulness of those early dye farms and factories stood in stark contrast to the beauty created by their ultimate product. So, drawbacks aside, the dyeing industry flourished, even amid secrecy, squalor, superstition, and often penalty of death to those who would reveal secret formulas or wear forbidden colors.

The discovery of new color sources and production methods spelled economic prosperity to many a city and financial ruin fell to those with outdated materials and methods.

BATIK AND NATURAL DYES

The art of batik made unique demands on natural dyes. Dyes used for batik must impart their colors without the use of heat because the more traditional boiling process would melt the fragile layer of wax, thus destroying the design. Only after all the color is in place can the fabric be boiled to remove the wax and permanently set the color. Cold water dyes also need to be colorfast so that a variety of hues can be used for each design without fear that they will run together or fade. Additionally, before cultures and continents were linked by trade routes, sources for these dyes needed to be found in the artisans' own backyard. Isolated peoples could not depend on berries and bark from the other side of the globe. Only with time did travel and trade expand the batik palette by allowing sources for

color production to be shared the world around.

Indigo was one of the most important colors of the early batik palette. First used in ancient India and Egypt, indigo was also cultivated in Indonesia, and from there spread to Java. Along with the various shades of blue, violet, lavender and black that came from indigo, the palette of the batik artisan usually included red, brown, and yellow. In Java, hues of red came from the bark and root of the morinda tree. Deep red was also derived from sappan wood. The soga tree was the source for brown and yellow while other shades of yellow came from safflower petals, turmeric root, and the boiled wood-shavings of the jackfruit tree.

Overlapping layers of dye could also produce a variety of colors. Yellow and blue combine to make green, yellow and red produce orange, and red and blue form violet. However, the traditional Javanese batiks were thought to be inferior if they contained overlapping colors so these blended colors were not often included.

ANILINE DYES

In 1856 a young British chemist named William Henry Perkin was experimenting with coal tar derivatives in an attempt to develop synthetic quinine. Quinine it wasn't, but the resultant purple-colored substance revolutionized the dyeing industry the world over. Perkin had inadvertently discovered aniline dye. His invention, which he called mauve or mauveine, led other scientists to develop additional formulas for synthetic-based dyes and soon colors derived from seashells, barks and berries faded into obscurity while new colors, colors produced in laboratory test tubes, took their place. Perkin's went on to build a factory to manufacture his discovery and aniline dye production became a thriving industry.

By the time knighthood was conferred on Sir Perkin in 1906, a wide variety of coal-tar derivative dyes were in use. These and subsequent aniline-based dyes created a palette of colors that were the mainstay of the dyeing industry for the next fifty years.

FIBER REACTIVE DYES

In 1956 the dyeing industry was once again revolutionized with the development of fiber-reactive dyes. The British company, Imperial Chemical Industries, Ltd., used petrochemicals to create a dye that bonds color molecules with fiber molecules. Instead of coating the outside of the fiber, the color now becomes an integral part of the fiber. The result is a long lasting color that can be used on almost all types of natural fibers including silk, cotton, hemp, viscose rayon, linen, flax, wool, and even wood, straw, and paper. Fiber-reactive dyes do not, however, work as well on synthetic fibers such as nylon, polyester, acetate, Mylar, and poly-blends.

Below: *Denpasar Market*
by Linda Kaun, 20"w x 16"h.

Immersion dyeing with vat dyes.

Right: *Amazon River*
by Mary Edna Fraser,
35"w x 115"h.

Direct dyeing with
fiber-reactive dyes.

Acid dyes and fiber-reactive dyes are variations of these petrochemical dyes and are now the most commonly used coloring agents for both commercial processes and for home crafting. They are particularly well suited to the needs of the batik artist because they are easy to use, provide intense, long-lasting color, do not require a boiling process, and can be used as a dip, or thickened to be used as paint.

BRANDS OF CHEMICAL DYES

There are many manufacturers of chemical dyes each with their own formulas, brand names, and instructions for usage. PRO-Chem, Ciba Acid Dyes, Fezan Batik Dyes, and Jacquard Acid Dyes, are common brands of acid dyes. The name Procion® has become so identified with fiber-reactive dye that it is often considered a generic term for the product even though it is really a manufacturer's brand name. Procion Dyes are also repackaged for other supply companies and sold under the names Createx Dye, Pro-Chem, and Dylon. Check your local art supply store for these and other brands of chemical dyes or look for them in mail order supply catalogs. Even though they all have a similar chemical base it is best not to intermix brands. Each dye has its own formula, its own set of directions, and requires a specific activating agent, all of which can produce differences in the dyeing process. Even different series within a given brand name, such as Procion's H-series, MX series, and M series, can vary and it is best to use only one specific dye product at a time.

Color Names

Every brand of dye has its own unique palette of colors. These colors are named and numbered for easy identification. Be aware that even when they are called by the same name, one brand's color can differ greatly from another's. For instance the *Sky Blue* of one brand may appear subtle and gray while the *Sky Blue* of another brand appears garishly bright. To select a hue, first check the color on the label of the package or study the manufacturer's color chart. These charts depict the full-intensity of each of the hues in that particular product line of dyes. Keep in mind that the small rectangles of color only approximate the actual color and, while they give you a general idea, will not identically match the dyed fabric.

Dye Lots

A dye lot is the entire amount of a given color-product that is produced at the same time from the same manufacturing procedures. Within every product there are differences from dye lot to dye lot of a given color. If you must match a color to a previously dyed one be sure to use the same dye lot for each of the dyebaths. Look for the dye lot code on the container of dye. Even when you use the same dye lot of color it is extremely difficult to recreate the exact recipe and timing of a particular color.

Photo by artist

Portrait of the Panhandle
by Arnelle Dow,
24"w x 24"h.

Immersion dyeing on linen.

Night Companion – Fabric Book
by Sara Austin,
19"w x 10"h (middle), 7"h (sides).

Resist, matte medium transfers,
over-dyeing, embroidery on velvet.

Photo by Monty Jessup

Non-Reactive Dyeing Equipment

Utensils and equipment made of certain metals such as tin, iron, aluminum, and galvanized steel, will trigger adverse chemical reactions when they come into contact with dyes and mordants. This unwanted reaction between the dye and metal may change the color of the dye or prevent the correct reaction between color and fiber. Avoid unwanted chemical reactions by using only non-reactive dyeing tools and equipment — those which will not interact with the dyes and mordants. Plastic, glass, enamelware, and stainless steel can all be used without a problem.

Dye Selection

What type of dye should you use to color your batiks? That depends on the fiber content of the fabric to be dyed, the hues you've selected, and the application method you intend to use. Personal preference is also a major factor. Most artists experiment until they find a particular brand of dye that works best for them and then use it exclusively — getting to know all the subtle intricacies and nuances involved in its application.

The fiber content of the fabric often determines the selection of the dye product. Cotton, viscose rayon, flax, hemp, and linen are made of cellulose fibers derived from vegetable matter. Use fiber-reactive dyes

with an alkali activator, acid dyes with salt activator, and direct dyes for these and all other cellulose fabrics. Silk is a protein fiber, woven from the unwound strands of silk worm cocoons. Use acid dyes with vinegar activator, basic dyes, or fiber-reactive dyes with a citric acid activator for best results on this delicate yet durable fabric. Wool, an animal hair, is also a protein fiber. It can be dyed with fiber-reactive dyes but some experts believe it is best to use acid dye for all types of wool fabrics. Synthetic fabrics such as nylon, polyester, synthetic rayon, acetate, and poly-blends do not absorb color nor do their molecular structures bond with the dye molecules of fiber-reactive dyes, so they require disperse dyes, or fabric inks and paints that coat the fibers rather than penetrate them.

Selection of the dye is also determined by the method to be used for its application. Full immersion dyeing is the more traditional method of coloring batik, and calls for dyes that can be mixed in quantity. Direct dyeing, the process of dipping portions of the fabric into the dye or painting the dyes directly onto the fabric, can be done with smaller amounts of dye or with various other fabric paints and inks.

The Dye Chart presents the major types of dye, their characteristics, brand names, and the appropriate fabrics for each.

There is no "one-size-fits-all" set of instructions for mixing and applying batik dyes. Directions vary from product to product and it is important to follow the manufacturer's specific directions in order to achieve optimum success with dyes. It is wise to make test swatches before dyeing the actual batik. Label each swatch with the dye recipe, the dye lot number, the timing of the dyebath, and the fabric content. Save swatches for future reference.

Follow all safety procedures when using dyes. Use non-reactive equipment and tools. Facemask and gloves are a must. Keep dyestuffs and chemicals away from children and animals and never use dyeing equipment for the preparation of food. Dispose of used dyes following manufacturer suggestions.

Using Natural Dyes

Gather natural dye sources yourself or purchase them from specialty shops and mail-order catalogues. Leaves, moss, bark, seedpods, flowers, vegetables, and insects are all used to produce dyes. Each color source requires its own special processing plus mineral or chemical color-setting additives called mordants. Often, the same color source can be used for a variety of different hues depending on the type of mordant added to the extracted pigment. For instance, hollyhock petals produce a wine red color with the addition of tin crystals and a dark brown hue when iron is added to the mixture. Purple crocus flowers create medium blue and turquoise hues with a mordant of alum and bright green when chrome is used. Purchase these mordants from a craft or weaving supply shop.

DYE CHART

DYE TYPE	CHARACTERISTIC	BRAND NAME	FABRICS
Dyes Classified by Content			
Natural Dyes	Vegetable, animal, and mineral sources for color combine with chemical and mineral mordants to produce rich, earthy colors. Procedures and mordants vary with each dye source. Steam or heat set.	Dharma Natural Dyes, Natural sources such as marigold blossoms, walnut hulls, Indian redwood bark	Cotton, hemp, linen, viscose rayon, flax, silk, wool, paper
Aniline Dyes	Coal-tar derivatives. Oxidation of the aniline creates the color.	Most aniline dyes are now obsolete	All cellulose fibers: flax, cotton, linen, hemp
Fiber-Reactive Dyes	Chemical reaction molecularly bonds color with fibers. Brilliant, long lasting and fade resistant. Requires the addition of chemicals to set color. Steam or heat set.	Procion (M,H, and MX series), Putnam Color and Dye, Fibrec, Dylon, Createx, PRO-Chem	Cotton, linen, flax, hemp, viscose rayon, silk, wool, paper
Acid Dyes	An exhaust dye that requires a mordant of household vinegar or tartaric acid for silk; ammonium sulfate or ammonium oxalate for cottons. Dyeing procedures vary depending on color and fabric. Steam or heat set.	PRO-Chem, Ciba Acid Dyes, Fezan Batik Dyes, Jacquard Acid Dyes, H Dupont, Schjeming Royal Silk Dyes	Silk, wool and other protein fiber, paper, cotton, flax, hemp, linen, viscose rayon
Basic Dyes	Dyes require a base solution of bicarbonate of soda or other alkali product and soda ash as a mordant Some fabrics must be steamed prior to dyeing. Steam or heat set.	Maxilon	Protein fibers of silk and wool. Cellulose fibers require different formula and dyeing method
Dyes Classified by Process			
Vat dyes	An exhaust dye with reactive properties. Requires total immersion of fabric. Color develops with heat or light. Test swatches a must. Steam or heat set.	Inkodye, Tionon, Tinosol	Cotton, hemp, linen, flax, silk, wool, wood, paper, and certain synthetics
Disperse Dyes	Chemical dyes for synthetic fabrics. Requires mordant of alkali and white vinegar. Popular for hosiery, lingerie, dancewear, and theatre costumes. Heat set.	Polydye, Aljo Acetate Nylon Dyes, Prospere Disperse Dyes	Orlon, dacron, mylar, acetate, polyester, poly-blends, plastics, nylon, acrylics
Azoic Dyes	Based on diazo reaction. Best on cellulose fibers. Needs no additional mordant.	Brentamin	Cotton, linen, hemp, flax, viscose rayon
Direct Dyes	Chemical reaction from steam is used to develop color. Less color fast than fiber-reactive dyes. Steam or heat set.	Deka-L, Aljo Cotton and Rayon Dyes, Diazol	Cotton, linen, hemp, viscose rayon, silk, wool
Other Colorants			
Fabric Inks	Coats the fibers but leaves a soft hand on fabrics. Alcohol or water base. Steam set.	Versatex Air Brush Ink, Dupont French Dyes	silk
Fabric Paints	Coats the fibers leaving a thicker hand on the fabric. Paint, spray, spatter, or sponge. Not suitable for submerge dyeing. Some paints require heat set or curing.	Jacquard Textile Colors, Deka, Lumiere Fabric Paint (metallic), Pebeo Silk Dye, Dye-na-Flow by Jacquard	Cotton, hemp, linen, flax, viscose rayon, silk, wool, nylon, acetate, polyester, paper, wood
Household Dyes	Direct and/or acid dyes. Mordants vary. Most require boiling. Do not work well in cold water. Heat set. Poor choice for batik.	Rit, Tintex, Putnam	Cotton, linen, hemp, flax, viscose rayon, silk, wool

Bird, by dmotoko, 14"w x 17"h.

Top: Marigold dyes
on Indonesian silk.

Bottom: Same motif using
dyes derived from Indian Redwood.

Photos by Kazutaka Tamura

While natural dyes are an integral part of the history and development of batik, most of today's artists use chemical dyes for their batik work. The artists who do use natural dyes have developed their own unique methods based on the particular raw materials available to them and the palette of colors they desire. If you are interested in working with natural dyes I suggest that you take some workshops in dyeing techniques and network with other artists who utilize natural dyes. Also, spend some time at your local library researching the details of various dyeing methods. There are many informative books on the subject, including some old out-of-print volumes that are every bit as useful as their modern counterparts.

The Japanese batik artist dmotoko makes and uses a variety of natural dyes. She plants marigolds in her garden and harvests the blossoms for a ready source of yellow, orange and green hues. She gathers some pigment materials and purchases less common sources such as the bark of the Indian redwood tree, buds of the Japanese pagoda tree, and packets of processed Indigo from commercial suppliers.

The following directions based on her method for using marigold blossoms will give you a preliminary understanding of natural dyes. If you do experiment with natural dyes follow all safety precautions. Test swatches are a must when using such variable products.

1 Marigold Dye Supplies.

2 Place flowers in a pot of water.

3 Remove flowers from pot.

4 Ease fabric into strained dye.

5 Blot unrinsed fabric.

6 Combine ratio of mordant and water.

Photos by Nicolas Kane

This hardy flower has been utilized as a medicine, flavoring, food coloring, and hair dye, as well as a fabric dye. The blossoms yield the strongest color when used fresh but they can also be dried and stored for long periods of time before the pigment is extracted. They produce colors ranging from yellow, gold, orange, deep rust, to dusty green and dark brown depending on the cooking time and the mordants used.

EXTRACTING THE PIGMENT

1. Gather blossoms. Use equal weight of blossoms to fabric.
2. Place blossoms into a non-reactive pot, add water (2 cups water to one cup blossoms), and bring to a boil. Do not cover with lid during the cooking process.
3. Add a pinch of bicarbonate of soda (baking soda) to the boiling liquid and reduce heat.
4. Simmer mixture until all pigment has discharged and blossoms have turned into a soft pulp. (Approximately 15 minutes.)
5. Remove blossoms from dye.
6. Simmer uncovered until dye liquid is reduced by 1/3. (approximately 15 minutes)
7. Strain dye into a non-reactive container and cool.

DYEING PROCEDURE FOR ALL COLORS

1. Fill a shallow non-reactive container with the dye.
2. Ease the fabric into the cooled dye, avoiding overlaps.
3. Soak fabric, rearranging it occasionally.
4. Blot or hang until damp dry.

Experiment with the timing of the dyebath, steeping the fabric longer for darker shades. When removed from the dye, the fabric will appear a soft tan color. The final hue will develop when the batik is soaked in a mordant bath.

Save the remaining dye in a jar with an airtight lid and store in a cool, dark place. To reuse, pour the dye into a non-reactive pan, bring to a boil, then cool it to room temperature. By keeping the dye separate from the mordant bath it can be used repeatedly for 7 to 10 days. Once a mordant mixes with the pigment, the shelf life of the dye is measured in hours.

7 Ease damp fabric into mordant bath.

8 Remove fabric from mordant.

9 Scrub with mild detergent and a soft brush.

10 Record dyeing information and swatches.

SUPPLIES

- Flower blossoms
- Bicarbonate of soda (baking soda)
- Chemical mordants (i.e. ferrous sulfate, wood vinegar iron, tin crystals, cream of tartar, alum)
- Non-reactive pot
- Non reactive measuring spoons
- Non-reactive stirrer and funnel
- Non reactive dyeing container
- Plastic clothesline and clothespins
- Kitchen timer
- Storage jars with lids
- Non-reactive strainer
- Protective gloves
- Face mask
- Synthropol or mild laundry soap

MORDANT BATH

After the batik has been soaked in the dye and damp dried, soak it in a mordant bath to develop the color. The chemical reaction between the pigment and the mordants changes the light tan of the dyed fabric to a variety of rich colors depending on the chemicals used and the timing of the bath. The following chart provides mordant recipes for a variety of marigold dye colors.

MORDANT PROCEDURE FOR ALL COLORS

1. Mix mordant in a shallow non-reactive container using the recipe chart. Prepare enough to completely cover the fabric.

2. Ease the damp-dried batik into the mordant bath and soak for 15 minutes. Rearrange fabric once or twice.

3. Remove batik from the mordant bath and lightly scrub each side with a drop of Synthropol or mild laundry soap and a soft brush to remove all traces of the chemical mordant.

4. Rinse and hang to dry.

The use of natural dyes may be more time consuming than using the common commercial brands of dyes but the reward for your patience is a variety of wonderfully luminous colors that cannot be achieved with chemical colorants.

MORDANT RECIPES FOR MARIGOLD DYES

Bright Yellow	1/4 teaspoon potassium aluminum sulfate (alum) to 1 cup warm water.
Reduced Yellow	1/4 teaspoon copper acetate to 1 cup warm water.
Reduced Green	1/8 teaspoon ferrous sulfate to 1 warm cup water.
Dark Brownish-Green	2 drops liquid wood-vinegar iron to 1 cup warm water.
Orange	1/8 teaspoon titanium dioxide crystals to 1 cup warm water.

1 Acid Dye Supplies.

2 Measure small amount of water.

3 Add established amount of dye to water.

4 Mix into paste.

5 Stir in water.

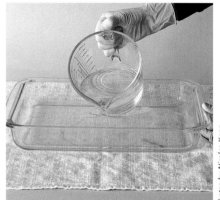

6 Measure established amount of water into dyeing container.

Photos by Nicolas Kane

Using Acid Dyes

Acid dyes are usually sold in powder form and are easy to mix and use. The only acid required for silk is household white vinegar. Cottons require the addition of salt. Shelf life of the dry dye powder is two to three years or more while a mixture of dye and vinegar will lose its potency in two or three weeks.

RATIO OF DYE, WATER, VINEGAR

The amounts of dye, water, and vinegar needed to dye silk, depend on the amount of fabric to be dyed, and the method to be used. For immersion dyeing weigh the dry fabric or determine the amount of liquid needed to cover the fabric. Check the manufacturer's recipe to determine the ratio of dye powder to the fabric weight or the amount of water

MIXING JACQUARD® ACID DYES

1. Establish the amount of water, dye powder, and vinegar.
2. Measure a very small amount of hot water into a measuring cup. (1 part water to 2 parts dye powder)
3. Add correct ratio of dye-powder and mix into a smooth paste.
4. Gradually stir in remaining cup of hot water.
   Mix thoroughly to dissolve.
5. Fill dyeing container with the correct ratio of cold water minus 1cup. (Use lukewarm water if you want to prevent the wax from cracking.)
6. Pour dye concentrate into water through cheesecloth-lined strainer.
7. Add vinegar to the dye and mix thoroughly. (1/4 cup vinegar per gallon of dye.)

7 Strain dye into water.

8 Add vinegar.

ACID DYE SUPPLIES

- Dyes
- Vinegar
- Kitchen timer
- Face mask and rubber gloves
- Non-reactive measuring cup and spoons
- Non-reactive stirrer
- Non-reactive dyeing container
- Non-reactive strainer and funnel
- Plastic clothes line and clothespins
- Storage jugs
- Assorted paint brushes
- Cheese cloth

9 Ease fabric into dye and rearrange fabric occasionally.

10 Record dyeing information and swatches in sketchbook.

DYEING METHODS FOR ACID DYES

Acid dyes can be applied in many ways. Fabric can be totally immersed in a dyebath or portions of the fabric can be selectively dipped in the color. Dye can also be painted onto walled-in sections or painted directly onto unwaxed areas of the fabric. Experiment with a variety of application methods, for each technique will add its own unique character to your batik work.

IMMERSION DYEING

1. Ease fabric into the dye.
2. Periodically turn and rearrange fabric.
3. Rinse fabric in cool water.
4. Line dry.

This traditional method of dyeing calls for totally submerging the waxed fabric in the dyebath. To avoid cracking the wax during the process use a container that is large enough to allow the batik to float freely and use lukewarm dye to keep the wax pliable but be careful not to make the dye so hot as to melt the wax out of the fabric. Batiks with cracks as part of the design should be colored in cold dyes to keep the wax brittle and the fissures open.

PARTIAL DYEING

1. Hold the designated area of fabric in the dyebath for the desired amount of time.
2. Dry the fabric and continue the waxing and dyeing process.

Capillary action will cause the dye to bleed into the dry areas of fabric creating a soft, blended look along the edges of the color.

WALLING-IN AREAS OF COLOR

1. Stretch the fabric on the frame, keeping the grain straight.
2. Outline areas of the design with thin lines of wax or gutta.
3. Apply the dye within the walled-in areas using a small, soft brush. Dry.
4. Seal the dyed sections of the design with wax, or create resist designs within the painted area.

This method allows you to create color combinations not possible with the overlapping colors of immersion dyebaths. Areas of the design are outlined with walls of gutta or wax and the dye is painted within the walled-in sections. The walls prevent the dye from spreading into other sections of the fabric. This creates a crisp, hard edge to the painted area.

Left: *Scroll Series: Back Yard in the Morning* by Arnelle Dow, 36"w x 48"h.

Direct and immersion dyeing.

Above: *The Old Strand Theatre, Key West* by Natalie Guess, 22"w x 28"h.

Immersion dyeing.

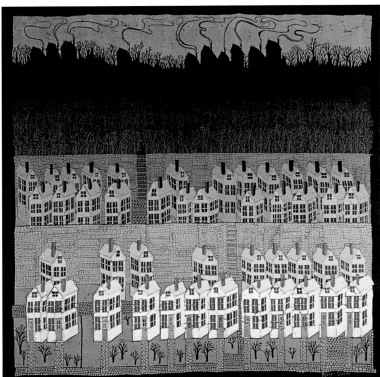

Houses at the Top
by Eloise Piper,
42"w x 42".

Immersion dyeing.

Photo by William Zinner

*After the
Gold Rush*
by Linda Gass,
26"w x 21"h.

Walled-in
areas of color,
machine quilted.

Photo by artist

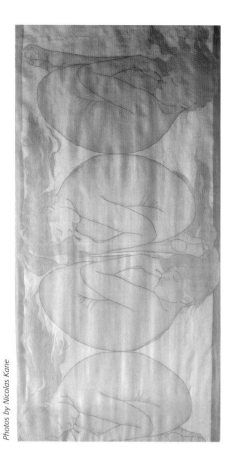

Above: *Figure Study* (and detail) by Eloise Piper, 42"w x 94"h.

Direct-dyed gradations of color on immersion-dyed China silk.

Right: *The Great Wave (after Hokusai)* by Lee Creswell, 16"w x 12"h.

Combination of soft-edged painting and hard-edged batik.

COLOR GRADATIONS

1. Stretch the batik on the frame keeping the grain straight.
2. Wall-in areas of the design.
3. Prepare small amounts of the dyes in varying strengths.
4. Paint the entire walled-in area with the lightest dye. Clear water can be substituted for the lightest value.
5. Apply a small amount of darker color along one side of the wet area. The dark dye will gradually bleed into the lighter color creating a soft gradation.
6. Lightly sweep a clean, dry brush over the blended area to smooth the color transition. (Optional)

The subtle gradation of a color gives the appearance of volume and is an interesting contrast to the more traditional flat pattern of batik. Light to dark gradations of a single color, or blends of two or more colors can be created within a walled-in area. Experiment with a variety of colors and color strengths, as well as with varying degrees of dampness. The wetter the fabric, the more the color will spread and soften.

PAINTING WITH THE DYE

1. Stretch the fabric on the frame keeping the tension even.
2. Mix a 10% solution of dye concentrate of each of the selected colors. (1 part dye to 10 parts water.) Pour mixtures into clean jars, cap, and label.
3. Pour small amounts of dye concentrates into custard cups and dilute to the desired color. Add a teaspoon of vinegar to each color.
4. Arrange the dye containers near the fabric. Keep some extra custard cups on hand for mixing other colors and a container of clean rinse water.
5. Test each color on a fabric swatch before painting it onto the fabric. Dry the swatch and adjust the color by adding

water to lighten and more dye concentrate to darken it.

6. Paint the dye onto the fabric. Allow the fabric to dry.

7. Apply wax to the dry sections of the design you wish to save. Paint the next color, dry the fabric, and apply the next layer of wax. Continue to paint, dry the fabric, and wax. In general, apply dyes from light to dark, overlapping the layers to form new colors.

Many batik artists use the dyes much as you would watercolor paints. Mix dyes in small custard cups and paint them onto the fabric with soft brushes or sponges. Apply wax to selected areas of dry fabric as the painting develops. This method allows for a spontaneous, free-flowing application of color and an intertwining of soft-edged painting with the hard-edged batik. A basic palette of primary dyes plus black can be used to extemporaneously mix other hues as the painting takes shape or colors can be mixed according to a pre-established palette. If you are planning to use the primary colors to mix all the other hues, remember to begin with cyan (blue), magenta (red) and yellow.

After the wax has been removed the batik can be re-worked with added layers of dye and wax, or embellished with paint, metallic guttas and other surface design materials. Discharge paste can be applied to create lighter sections of the design.

STEAM-SETTING THE ACID DYE

While ironing is often all it takes to set the dyes, they can also be steam-set to further brighten the colors and assure their colorfastness. Steam setting is particularly recommended for clothing and wearable accessories. Directions for wax removal and steam setting are presented in chapter six.

Ancient Chumash #1 by Bernadette DiPietro, 16"w x 12"h.

Direct dyeing on handmade paper.

Photo by artist

Photo by William Zinner

River Reflections, by Eloise Piper, 42"w x 48"h.

China silk was folded, waxed, immersion-dyed, ironed, unfolded, waxed and overdyed.

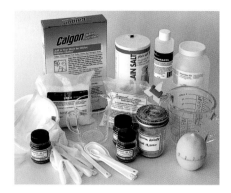

1 Fiber-Reactive Dye Supplies.

2 Pour the measured amount of water into the dyeing container.

3 Dissolve the measured amount of salt into a cup of hot water.

4 Pour the dissolved salt into the dyeing container.

5 Measure a small amount of hot water into a measuring cup.

6 Add the determined ratio of dye powder.

7 Mix into a paste.

8 Add hot water to dye paste.

9 Stir dye concentrate into the dyeing container.

Photos by Nicolas Kane

Using Fiber-Reactive Dyes

The following recipes and directions are for use on cellulose fibers such as cotton, linen and rayon. If you are dyeing silk, you will need different chemical additives. Check the manufacturer's directions or purchase dyes that are specially formulated for silk. Fiber-reactive dyes for cellulose fibers require the addition of several chemicals to aid in the dyeing process. Calsolene oil or Urea help to dissolve the dye granules and keep the fabric moist while the dye reacts with the fiber. Water softener neutralizes any harmful mineral content in the water. Table salt or Glauber's Salt is added to enhance the color.

The dye also requires an activa-

10 Ease fabric into the dye.

11 Rearrange fabric occasionally.

FIBER-REACTIVE DYE SUPPLIES

- Dyes
- Urea (wetting agent)
- Calsolene oil (wetting agent)
- Table salt (color enhancer)
- Calgon (water softener)
- Baking soda or soda ash (alkali)
- Synthropol (detergent)
- Protective gloves and face mask
- Dyeing container
- Non-reactive measuring spoons and cups
- Non-reactive buckets, bowls, jars
- Non-reactive stirrer
- Kitchen timer
- Plastic clothes pins and clothes line
- Plastic wrap
- Storage jugs and plastic funnel
- Quart canning jars with lids
- Sodium alginate (optional thickener)

12 Dissolve the determined amount of soda ash in a cup of hot water.

13 Remove batik from dyebath.

14 Stir in soda ash solution.

15 Return fabric to the dyebath and rearrange fabric occasionally.

tor to trigger the molecular reaction of dye and fabric. Soda ash, a common activator for cellulose fabrics, can be mixed in quantity ahead of time and stored for months. Once it is added to the pigment the solution remains at full strength for only four to six hours. You can lengthen the life of the dye by soaking the fabric in the activator prior to dyeing and omitting the activator from the mixed dyes.

Procion MX fiber-reactive dyes and Dharma fiber-reactive dyes are both fast to react and do not require heat during the dyeing process.

Think safety! Always use gloves and a mask when handling the dyes and chemicals. Clean up spills immediately. A dampened paper towel placed under the mixing area will catch spilled dye powders and chemicals and prevent them from becoming airborne. It is strongly recommended *not* to use fiber-reactive dyes in the kitchen. Never smoke or eat while working with the dyes.

Presented here are the most common methods for using fiber-reactive dyes: immersion dyeing, dyeing in the washing machine, and direct dyeing. Also discussed are over-dyeing, and creating gradations of a single hue.

RATIO OF DYE, WATER, CHEMICALS

The amounts of dye, water, and chemicals you will need depend on the amount of fabric to be dyed, and the method to be used. Weigh the dry fabric or determine the amount of liquid needed to immerse it. Use as little water as possible because the dye reacts with the water as well as the fabric. Check the manufacturer's recipe for the ratio of dye powder and chemical additives for that amount of water. The dyes and chemicals can be measured or weighed. Record the amounts of water, dye powder, salt, Calsolene oil, and soda ash before preparing the dye.

IMMERSION DYEING WITH FIBER-REACTIVE DYES

Immersion dyeing is a traditional method for dyeing batiks. Florida artist Muffy Clark Gill and Linda Kaun, an artist living in Indonesia, share their expertise. Beatrice Colman, professor of Fiber Arts at California State University Northridge, reviewed the information and her suggestions and clarifications are also included.

MIXING THE DYE

1. Dissolve the established ratio of table salt in a cup or two of hot water. (1 cup salt per 1 gallon of dye solution.) Cool. Pour the dissolved salt into the dyeing container.
2. Measure a small amount of tap water into a dry measuring cup. (Use approximately 1 part water to 2 parts powdered dye).
3. Carefully add the correct ratio of dye powder and mix into a smooth paste.
4. Fill the cup with hot water and stir to dissolve the dye paste.
5. Pour mixture into the dyeing container. Add remaining amount of cool water.
6. Stir in Calsolene oil. (2 teaspoons per 3 gallons of dye)

Never pour liquid directly into the dry dye powder for this will cause a small explosion, sending the powder airborne. Instead, carefully add the dry powder to a small amount of liquid and stir to form a paste before adding more liquid. Always wear gloves and a mask when working with dry dye powders.

DYEING THE FABRIC

1. Ease fabric into the dye. Make sure fabric is totally immersed.
2. Rearrange fabric occasionally to assure an even color. Dye for 10 to 40 minutes or more depending on desired color.

Photo by artist

Pool IV, by Karen Perrine, 41"w x 53.5"h.
Whole cloth image created from multiple dyeing, resist, painting and sewing processes.

EXTENDING THE REACTION TIME

1 Place unrinsed batik on a sheet of plastic wrap.

2 Cover with a top sheet of plastic wrap.

3 Seal edges of plastic wrap.

Photos by Nicolas Kane

ACTIVATING THE DYE

1. Dissolve the required amount of soda ash in a cup or two of hot water. (1/3 cup of soda ash per 3 gallons of dye solution.) Cool.

2. Remove the batik from the dye and stir the soda ash solution into the dye.

3. Return the batik to the dye and soak for 30 to 60 minutes or more, rearranging the fabric occasionally. (The longer the soak, the darker the color). Dye potency will last 4-6 hours once the soda ash is mixed into the pigment.

4. Rinse the batik in cold water and line dry.

EXTENDING THE REACTION TIME

Sandwich the wet, unrinsed fabric between two sheets of plastic wrap and allow it to sit for a few hours. This keeps the fabric wet and allows the molecular reaction to continue, creating a deeper color.

ACTIVATING THE UNDYED FABRIC

If the short shelf life of activated dye is an inconvenience, pre-soak the fabric in a solution of activator and water. The fabric can then be waxed and dyed without further use of an activator.

1. Establish the amount of soda ash and water. (1cup soda ash per 1 gallon water.)

2. Dissolve the soda ash in a cup or two of hot tap water.

3. Pour mixture into a dyeing container. Add the remaining amount of water.

4. Ease clean fabric into the solution and soak for 15 to 20 minutes. Turn occasionally.

5. Do not rinse the fabric. Squeeze out excess liquid and line dry. The fabric is now ready to be waxed and dyed.

6. Pour remaining soda ash solution into a clean container. Cap, label, and store in cool, dark place. Solution can be reused for 2-4 months.

ACTIVATING THE UNDYED FABRIC

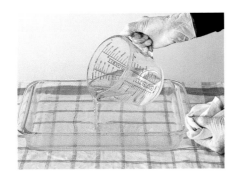

1 Pour a cup or two of hot water into dyeing container.

2 Dissolve the required amount of soda ash.

3 Ease fabric into solution and rearrange occasionally.

Photos by Nicolas Kane

DYEING THE PRE-TREATED FABRIC

1. Establish the ratios of dye, salt, water, and Calsolene oil based on the weight of the dry fabric to be dyed or the amount of water needed to immerse it.

2. Dissolve the required amount of table salt in 1 or 2 cups of hot tap water. (1-cup salt per 1-gallon dye solution) Pour into dyeing container.

3. Measure small amount of hot tap water into a dry measuring cup. (1part water to 2 parts powdered dye).

4. Add dye powder and mix into a smooth paste. (Follow the manufacturer's suggested ratio of dye to liquid for the desired shade.)

5. Fill cup with hot water and stir to dissolve the dye paste. Pour into the dyeing container.

6. Add the remaining amount of cold tap water.

7. Stir in some Calsolene oil. (2-teaspoons per 3-gallons water)

8. Ease the dry, pre-treated fabric into dye. Rearrange occasionally to assure an even color. Dye 10-40 minutes or more.

9. Rinse fabric in cold water and line dry.

Photo by artist

Northern Woods
by Helen Carkin, 30"w x 18.5"h.

Impetus
by Noel Dyrenforth, 60cm x 70cm.

Dyeing in the Washing Machine

Katherine Drew Dilworth creates batik designs on cotton and linen clothing. Here is her method for dyeing the garments in the washing machine. She buys dyes and chemicals in bulk and suggests pool supply companies as a source for the soda ash and bakery supply stores for 80-pound bags of table salt. She also adds Synthropol to the dyebath.

Photo by Norman Watkins

Machine-dyed dress by Katherine Drew Dilworth.

PRE-DAMPENING THE FABRIC

Prevent streaking by "wetting out" the fabric before dyeing it.

1. Weigh the dry fabric and record the poundage in your sketchbook. You will need this dry weight in order to determine the ratio of dye, water, and chemicals.

2. Put the garments through a gentle rinse and spin cycle.

3. Remove them from the washer before filling the washer and mixing the dye.

DETERMINE RATIO OF DYE, WATER AND CHEMICALS

1. Based on the manufacturer's suggested ratio of liquid to dry fabric, determine the amount of liquid needed to dye fabric.

2. Select the color and determine the ratio of dye powder for the measured amount of water based on the manufacturer's recipe for that particular hue.

3. Also determine the amounts of the chemical additives based on the amount of dye liquid.

4. Record all information in your sketchbook.

MIXING THE DYE

1. Fill washing machine with correct amount of cold water. Measure the water by the gallon before pouring it into the washing machine. (Mark gallon levels on a large bucket to speed the process).

2. Don gloves and mask.

3. Measure a small amount of water into a dry container. (Approximately 1 part water to 2 parts powdered dye). Carefully add the determined amount of dye powder and mix to form a smooth paste.

4. Mix the dye paste with 3 to 4 cups of hot water in a large plastic container such as a quart yogurt container. Stir.

5. Pour dissolved dye into the washer. Never pour dry dye powder directly into the washer for it may cause the powder to become airborne.

Machine-dyed hat and dress
by Katherine Drew Dilworth.

Machine-dyed clothing and accessories
by Katherine Drew Dilworth.

6. Add salt to the water.
(1cup salt per 1 gallon water)

7. Add 2 tablespoons of
Synthropol.

8. Agitate 5 minutes to dissolve
salt and detergent.

MACHINE DYEING THE FABRIC

1. Place damp garments into the
washer and gently agitate 5
minutes.

2. Turn off the machine and
allow the garments to soak
for 10 minutes.

3. Agitate the clothing for 2
minutes. Soak for 10 minutes.

4. Repeat procedure, continuing
to agitate (2 minutes) and soak

(10 minutes) for 40 minutes. If
the agitation causes the wax to
crack more than you intended,
try reducing the churning time
between soak intervals.

ACTIVATING THE DYE

1. Dissolve soda ash in 8 cups of
very hot tap water. (1/3-cup
soda ash per 3 gallons dye
water). Add the dissolved soda
ash to the dyebath being
careful not to pour it directly
onto the fabric. Agitate 2
minutes and soak for another
40 minutes. Agitate the load
twice during this soak period.

2. Rinse thoroughly and spin dry.

3. Line dry. Streaking may occur
if the fabric has not been
rinsed thoroughly.

Wax must be removed completely for
a garment to be wearable. Iron out as
much of the wax as possible. To
remove all traces of the wax,
Katherine takes the dried clothing to
a commercial dry-cleaner who
charges by the pound. After the wax
is removed she gives the clothing a
final washing in hot water and
Synthropol to remove all excess dye
before rinsing the clothing and
drying in the clothes dryer. The
residue of chemical solvents can be
irritating to the skin, so use gloves to
handle the dry-cleaned clothing
before it is washed.

DIRECT DYEING

Dye can be painted onto areas of the batik using a variety of methods. Watercolor painting techniques can be used for a fresh, spontaneous effect. Large solid areas of color can be applied with a soft brush. Dye can also be dripped, dribbled, splashed, sponged and sprayed onto the fabric. Portions of the fabric can be dipped into the dye or walled-in sections of the design can be selectively colored. Experiment to find the best method for you. Remember to make those dye swatches and record all pertinent information.

MIXING THE CHEMICAL WATER

1. Measure one-cup hot water into quart canning jar.
2. Add 1/2 cup of urea and stir to dissolve.
3. Add 1/2 teaspoon Calgon or other softener. Stir to dissolve.
4. Stir in three cups cold water.
5. Cover with lid, label with formula, poison warning and date. Store in a cool, dark cabinet.

Begin by mixing a quart of chemical water. Use small amounts as needed and store the remainder in a cool, dark place. Mixture will last for many months if it is not contaminated with dye or activator.

THICKENING THE CHEMICAL WATER

If you prefer a thicker consistency of dye, sodium alginate can be added to the chemical water. It comes in two thicknesses; a high viscosity for use on cottons and a low viscosity for use on silk.

1. Sprinkle one teaspoon of sodium alginate into the chemical water, a little at a time, stirring constantly to dissolve the lumps.

MIXING & THICKENING CHEMICAL WATER

1 Add 1/2 cup of urea to a cup or two of hot water.

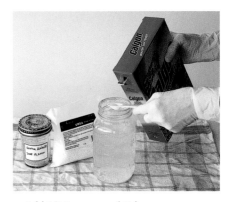

2 Add 1/2 teaspoon of Calgon.

3 To Thicken, sprinkle 1-teaspoon sodium alginate into chemical water.

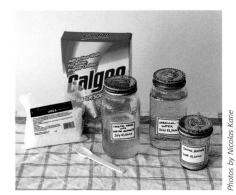

4 Cover and label.

Photos by Nicolas Kane

2. Gradually stir in more thickener as needed. Be careful not to over thicken. Cover, label, and let the thickened mixture sit overnight.
3. Stir before adding it to dyes.

PAINTING WITH ACTIVATED DYES

The following directions for preparing and painting with the dyes are based on the techniques of Christa Corner, Robin Paris, and Lee Creswell, batik artists living in the United Kingdom. Christa uses a combination of free-style painting and batik on a variety of papers such as handmade Chinese paper and tissue papers. Lee combines free-style painting and batik on silk while Robin prefers cotton. Even though their methods are similar, they have each developed their own special nuances to the procedure and their end results are very different from one another.

Stretch fabric on a frame or arrange the paper on absorbent unprinted newsprint. Some prefer to tape the paper to the work surface while others like Christa allow the movement of the untaped paper to interplay with the evolving design. Place a large jar of rinse water, an assortment of watercolor brushes or bamboo calligraphy brushes, and clean rags near at hand. Always make test swatches before applying the colors to the fabric or paper.

MIXING A 10% DYE SOLUTION

1. Don mask and gloves.
2. Measure 10 tablespoons hot water into a small jar.
3. Measure 1/2 tablespoon of the hot water into a separate container.
4. Carefully add 1 tablespoon of dye powder and mix into paste.
5. Stir in a pinch of table salt.
6. Add remaining amount of hot water and stir to dissolve. Pour into jar, cap tightly and label.

Mix a small concentrated amount of each of the selected colors. Information on combining colors and color arrangements can be found in chapter 4. Beatrice Colman suggests making a 10% concentrate solution (1 part dye powder to 10 parts water) of each color and thinning and activating smaller amounts as needed. The concentrate will keep for 2-4 weeks unrefrigerated. The following fiber-reactive dye directions are for use on cellulose fabrics.

DILUTING & ACTIVATING THE DYES

1. Pour a small amount of dye concentrate into a small wide-mouth container such as a custard cup.
2. Add 1/8-cup chemical water and a small amount of cold tap water to create the desired dye strength.
3. Measure a few teaspoons of hot water into a dry container and carefully add 1/2 teaspoon of soda ash. Stir to dissolve.
4. Mix soda solution into dye.
5. Use prepared dye immediately

APPLYING THE ACTIVATED DYES

1. Arrange the cups of dye on a tray near the fabric or paper.
2. Brush the dye onto the fabric using a variety of watercolor

Lower Oxararfass, Iceland, by Lee Creswell, 9"w x 14"h.
Direct dyeing.

techniques. Blend colors, let one color run into another, or sprinkle salt on a selected area to create a textural effect. Be experimental!

3. Always wash the brush in clean water before dipping it into a different color to avoid contaminating the dye.
4. Dry the fabric before covering

areas of the design with wax.

5. Continue to build multiple layers of wax and dye.

A hairdryer speeds the drying time if the fabric is free of wax. Once the wax is applied, heat from a dryer may melt the wax unless extreme care is taken to avoid over-heating the waxed design.

Kite Series
by Jim Nordmeyer,
24"w x 24"h.

Subtle gradation of
color created with
direct dyeing.

PAINTING ON PRE-ACTIVATED FABRIC

To extend the life of the dyes, treat the fabric or paper with activator before applying the dye. Dyes are then mixed without the addition of activator. Unused portions of the unactivated dye can be stored and reused for many weeks. See page 77 for directions on pretreating fabric with activator. If you are using paper, brush the activator solution over the entire sheet. Dry.

1. Stretch the activated fabric on the frame keeping the grain straight and the tension even.
2. Select the palette and mix the dyes from the concentrates omitting the alkali activator.
3. Apply dye with brushes as you would watercolor paints.
4. Wax the dried sections of the design you wish to retain. Continue painting and waxing the batik.

PAINTING SOLID AREAS WITH ACTIVATED DYE

Mary Edna Fraser uses the direct dyeing method to color her aerial landscape paintings because her work is far too large to immerse in a dyebath. She stretches the long lengths of silk over sawhorses and secures them in place. For smaller pieces, stretch the fabric on a frame making sure the grain is straight and the tension is even. Mix enough dye to cover the designated area. Mary

1 Applying wax outlines.

2 Painting the lightest of the colors.

3 Shading with a deeper hue.

Photos by Nicolas Kane

Edna mixes each hue by the gallon to assure a color consistency throughout the painting. While you will probably not need that quantity, you will need approximately 2 cups of dye per yard of average weight fabric. If you prefer a thicker dye consistency, use chemical water that has been thickened with sodium alginate.

Paint the dyes onto the fabric with an absorbent brush. Each solid area of color must be applied without interruption. If the fabric dries, the overlap of dry color and freshly painted dye will create a dark line.

PARTIAL DYEING, WALLING-IN, AND SOFT GRADATIONS OF DYE

Many of the procedures described in the section on acid dyes can also be used for applying fiber-reactive dyes. Experiment with painting the color onto walled-in areas of the design or create color gradations and soft-edged areas of color. Just remember to include the activator either in the dyes or on the unpainted fabric before the dye is applied.

Pacific Revenge (detail), by Robin Paris, 22.5"w x 33.5"h.

Direct dyes applied to walled-in design.

Photo by artist

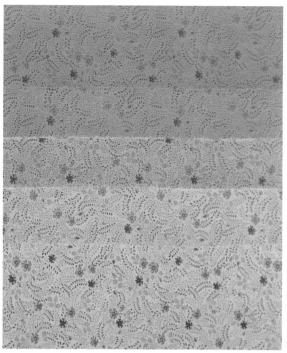

Left: *Overdyeing.*

Above: *Gradations of one hue.*

Photos by Nicolas Kane

OVER DYEING

Over dyeing is the process of re-dyeing a previously colored fabric. It can be used to change selected areas of color within a completed batik or to transform the entire batik. Over dyeing can also be used on commercially colored fabrics. Prints, stripes, woven designs, and solid colored fabric can all be over dyed to subtly modify their intensity and value or to totally change their original hues. Quilters particularly enjoy this method of altering the original hues and values of a fabric while at the same time keeping it compatible with undyed or previously dyed portions of the same fabric.

Select the type of dye you prefer and mix it according to instructions. Experimenting with various application methods, apply the dye to the fabric. Heat-set the dyes with steam or iron following the directions in chapter 6.

GRADATIONS OF ONE HUE

1. Cut the fabric into the desired number of pieces.
2. Following the immersion dyeing directions, mix up dye in the darkest shade of the color progression.
3. Fill the dyeing container with enough dye to completely cover one piece of fabric.
4. Place a piece of fabric in the dye. Turn occasionally to assure even coloration.
5. Dye for 10-30 minutes or more. Add soda ash. Soak for 30 minutes or more.
6. Remove fabric from the dye, rinse and dry. (Fabric will dry a few shades lighter).
7. Repeat for the second piece of fabric, lightening the dye strength and shortening the dyeing time as needed. Add water to the dye if the fabric remains too dark and more dye concentrate if it is too light.
8. Dye the next piece of fabric, adjusting the color strength and shortening the time again. Continue adjusting the dye and shortening the dyeing time for each remaining piece of fabric.
9. Record all measurements in your sketchbook.

Quilters often create a variety of color gradations using a single color of dye. Light to dark gradations can be used to alter a solid fabric or one with a printed or woven design. Always create a series of fabric swatches to determine the correct dye strength and timings before beginning work on the final pieces of fabric. It may take some time to establish the exact recipe for each gradation, but time spent on the swatches will assure success with the actual fabric pieces. Record all information in your sketchbook.

Linda's Toaster Dream: Breakfast for the Nuclear Family by Linda M. Scholten, 17"w x 20.5"h.

Direct and discharge dyeing with embroidery and buttons.

Photo by artist

Discharge Dyeing

A unique departure from the traditional dyeing process, discharge dyeing uses a bleaching agent to lighten or remove color from designated areas of fabric. After the bleaching paste has produced the desired amount of lightness, the fabric is thoroughly washed and rinsed in vinegar to halt any further bleaching action. Select a solid colored fabric or one that has a printed or woven design. You can also purchase fabrics that are colored with fugitive, easy to remove color. These special discharge fabrics are available at art supply stores and through mail order sources.

Discharge dyeing can be combined with batik, direct painting, and over-dyeing to create an unlimited variety of striking effects. Premixed bleaching agents such as Inko Discharge Paste and Jacquard Discharge Paste can be purchased at an art supply store. These can be used on most natural fabrics. You can also create a household bleach paste from thickening agents and liquid laundry bleach. This homemade mixture is too strong for delicate silks and rayon but works well on cotton and cotton blends.

JACQUARD DISCHARGE PASTE

1. Stretch the fabric on a frame, keeping the grain straight.
2. Apply the discharge paste to the selected areas of the design.
3. Thin the mixture with water as needed to allow the paste to penetrate the fabric. Allow the fabric to dry thoroughly.
4. Iron the fabric with a steam iron set on the lowest setting. The more steam the better. The color will leave the fabric at this stage. Ironing will create chemical vapors that have a very strong smell. Be sure to wear a mask or a vapor/mist respirator.
5. Wash the fabric in Synthropol and rinse.
6. Soak the fabric in a solution of 1 part vinegar to 4 parts water to neutralize the paste and prevent further bleaching.
7. Rinse with water and line dry.

Always experiment on swatches of the selected fabric before beginning work on the final piece. Be sure to wear protective mask and gloves.

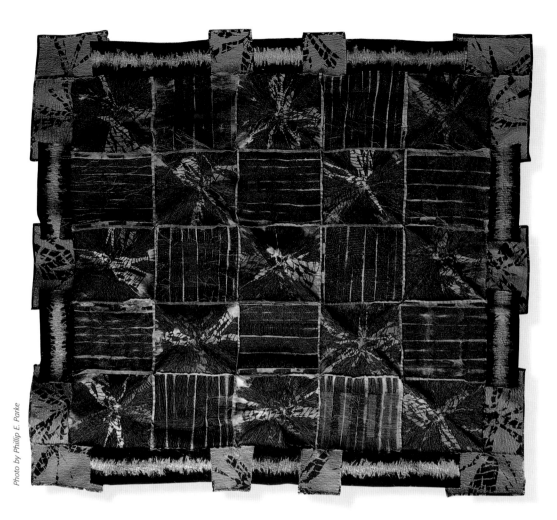

African Violets
by Rosanna Lynne Welter,
54"w x 54"h.

Discharge and hand
painted shibori fabrics
with tucks, raw edges,
and machine quilting.

HOUSEHOLD BLEACH PASTE

Mix the water, Calgon, and sodium alginate together in a clean, glass jar. Adjust the amount of alginate for the desired thickness. Add the bleach and mix well with a non-metallic stirrer. Label the jar with the recipe, a poison warning, and the date. Cap with an airtight lid and store in a cool, dark place. Allow the mixture to sit overnight to thoroughly dissolve the thickener.

1. Stretch the fabric on the frame keeping the grain straight and the tension even.

2. Apply the bleaching solution to the pattern or the background area using a brush, small squeeze bottle with a narrow tipped applicator, or spatula.

3. Time the bleaching action according to the results of your swatch experiments. 5 minutes or less should be enough for most fabrics. Don't over bleach.

4. Rinse the fabric.

5. Soak fabric in a bath of 1 part vinegar to 4 parts water to neutralize the bleaching action.

6. Wash in Synthropol, rinse and line dry.

This formula is for sturdy cottons and linens. Always experiment with test swatches to establish the correct timing before working on the actual piece. The color in some fabrics will not discharge completely, but most fabrics can be lightened enough to allow for interesting contrasts in the design. Discharged areas can be recolored with various resist and hand painting techniques.

HOUSEHOLD BLEACH PASTE RECIPE

1/2 cup hot water
1/4 teaspoon Calgon
1/2 cup liquid bleach

1-teaspoon sodium alginate
(optional)
Jar with tight lid
White vinegar

Dye Storage and Disposal

Some dyes can be saved and reused while others loose their potency in a matter of hours. Check the manufacturer's directions for information on the storage and reuse of the dyes. If you plan to save dye, use a wide mouth, non-reactive funnel to transfer the dye from the dyeing vat into a clean container such as a gallon milk jug. Label the container with a poison warning, the dye brand and color, mixing recipe, date, and shelf-life information. Seal with a tight lid and store in a cool, dark place out of the reach of children. Should mold form on the surface of the dye, pour the dye through a cheesecloth-lined strainer before reusing. Keep in mind that the dye may look rich and strong but have little pigment strength, so always test the color on a fabric swatch before reusing.

Do not automatically pour used dye down the drain or on the lawn. Certain dyes and chemicals can damage septic systems, water supplies, and the earth. Dispose of all dyes following manufacturer's suggestions or call your local poison center for instructions.

In Summary

Experience is the best teacher when it comes to mixing and using dyes. No simple, blanket set of directions will apply to all dyes for there are so many different types of dye, each with its own chemicals, specific additives, and dyeing techniques. Even within a specific brand of dye there is variation depending on the content of the fabric to be colored and the technique used.

Nothing is a substitute for hands-on experience under the guidance of an expert, so I suggest you take some dye-related workshops at your local art center and also do some preliminary research at your local library. Batik, tie-dye, and silk painting are a few of the crafting procedures that utilize dyes. Familiarize yourself with various dye products and methods by following the manufactures' directions and testing all products on sample swatches. After you have become familiar with various types of dye and dyeing methods you will be able to confidently select the ones that you prefer. Experience also allows you to add your own special nuances to the procedures, subordinating the technical aspects to your personal vision.

Harbour Patterns, by Ruth Holmes.

1 Sandwich batik between clean unprinted newsprint.

2 Iron until paper no longer absorbs wax.

Photos by Nicolas Kane

1. Protect the ironing board with a covering of heavy cotton. I prefer untreated cotton canvas.

2. Cover the ironing board with a thick pile of newspaper. Unfold each sheet and arrange to form a pad, 8-10 sheets thick.

3. Set iron on a dry setting, adjusting temperature to match the fabric to be ironed.

4. Cut two sheets of unprinted newsprint. Cover the top layer of newspaper with one of the sheets.

5. Place the batik on top of the newsprint. Smooth out wrinkles.

6. Cover the batik with the other sheet of unprinted newsprint.

7. Iron the surface of the paper. Be careful not to touch the bare fabric with the hot iron for this might burn or pucker the material. Keep the iron constantly moving to avoid scorching the wax and the fabric. The papers will absorb the wax and turn translucent with the residue.

8. Change the newspaper padding and the two sheets of clear newsprint often. Continue ironing until the papers no longer show traces of wax.

This method uses inexpensive, readily available supplies and is the safest of the wax-removal methods. It does however produce pungent fumes from the melting wax so it is important to work in a well-ventilated area and wear a nose/mouth mask. Use an exhaust fan and if you find the fumes particularly irritating, wear a respirator mask.

The key to successful wax removal by ironing is to change the newspaper and newsprint often. As soon as the papers become translucent with melted wax, exchange them for clean ones. It is more economical to build a thick, absorbent pad of inexpensive newspaper and top it with the two "sandwich" sheets of costlier unprinted newsprint. When handling the inky newspaper be careful not to spread ink from your hands to the clean paper or the batik.

It usually takes only two sheets of clean newsprint to entirely sandwich a small batik. If your batik is too large to fit between two sheets, work in sections, moving the fabric and adjusting the position of the papers as necessary to reach all areas of the fabric.

IRONING SUPPLIES

- Iron
- Extension cord
- Ironing board (or padded table)
- Heavy cotton ironing board cover
- Scissors
- Face mask
- Exhaust fan
- Lots of old newspaper
- Roll of unprinted newsprint

If the batik is not to be used for a garment or a wearable accessory, it is sometimes useful to leave a slight residue of wax in the fabric. The wax provides body to the fabric and also serves as a protective coating.

The heat from the ironing process is often all that is needed to permanently set the dyes. If the dyes require a steam bath to set the pigments, the batik is now ready for that step. If the fabric must be entirely free of wax, steam-set the color and then dry clean to remove the remaining residue.

1. Place a large pot of water on medium-high heat.
2. Add a tablespoon or two of mild laundry soap (soap helps free the wax from the fabric.)
3. Place batik in the water. Make sure there is room enough for the batik to float freely.
4. Bring the water to a boil. Stir occasionally to open any folds or twists.
5. Remove the fabric from the pot to the plate. When cool, hang up to dry.
6. Repeat process two or three times as necessary.

This traditional method of removing all traces of wax is an excellent method if you are sure that the dyes are colorfast. It takes no special supplies or equipment. However, it does require that the batik is able to withstand heat and water. Fugitive dyes will bleed and run and some will even discharge altogether, ruining many hours of laborious work. Always experiment with dye-swatches for all the colors used in a particular batik before committing a piece to this irreversible process. Some artists iron the batik to remove as much wax as possible before boiling the fabric while others do not because they believe that ironing embeds the wax more tightly into the fibers. Ironed fabric can also be steam set before the boiling to make the dyes completely colorfast. If you have any doubt as to the outcome of this procedure, do not jeopardize your hard work but choose instead to have the batik professionally dry-cleaned to remove the final traces of wax-residue.

BOILING SUPPLIES

- Large pot
- Stove or hotplate
- Long-handled stirrer
- Plate
- Mild laundry soap
- Clothesline and clothespins

Disposing of the Waxy Water

After each boiling, let the water cool. The wax will coagulate and float to the surface where it can be removed and disposed of safely. Never pour hot, waxy water down the drain. The wax will clog the pipes as it cools.

To Market, To Market
by Linda Kaun,
30"w x 22"h.

The artist uses the boiling method to remove the wax from her batiks.

Photo by artist

1 Place batik on top of a sheet of brown craft paper and two sheets of newsprint.

2 Cover with two sheets of newsprint.

3 Roll into a cylinder, flatten and secure roll with tape.

4 Coil and secure with twine.

Photos by Nicolas Kane

Steam Setting the Color

Steam is used to heat-set the dyes after the wax has been removed from the fabric. The heat and moisture of the steam render the dyes permanent and colorfast and also enhance the intensity of the colors. This is a recommended step for batiks that are to be used for garments and wearable accessories, as well as for batiks colored with silk dyes, acid dyes, and certain fiber-reactive dyes. After the colors are steam-fixed, professional dry-cleaning, or boiling can be employed to remove any remaining traces of wax residue.

Steam kettles designed especially for this process can be purchased at specialty art-supply shops, but a standard enameled canning kettle from the local hardware store is just as effective. Once you have used the kettle for setting the dyes, do not use it for the preparation of foodstuffs.

PREPARING THE BATIK

1. Iron out the batik to remove the majority of the wax. Spread out a large piece of brown wrapping paper. On top place a sheet or two of newsprint. Smooth the batik on top of the newsprint leaving a border on all sides.

2. Cover with two sheets of clear newsprint.

3. Loosely roll up the layers to form a tube, smoothing the batik as you roll. Flatten the tube and secure it with tape at either end and at two or three points along the length.

4. Coil the flattened tube and firmly secure it with twine.

1 Center lid on towel. Place rounds of newspaper under lid.

2 Wrap lid in towel and secure with safety pins.

3 Invert canning rack in bottom of kettle.

4 Add water.

5 Drop in a couple of pennies or a few small pebbles.

6 Places rounds of newspaper (foil in center) on the rack.

Photos by Nicolas Kane

PREPARING THE STEAM KETTLE

1. Cut 12-15 sheets of newspaper into circles that fit inside the lid of the kettle. These will absorb the moisture that condenses on the inside of the lid. Stack the cut papers on a towel. Cover with the lid.

2. Wrap the lid in the towel and secure it with safety pins.

3. Invert the canning rack in the bottom of the kettle.

4. Add water to within 2 inches of the top of the rack.

5. Drop pennies or pebbles into the kettle.

6. Cut 12-15 circles of newspaper and one circle of aluminum foil to fit inside the kettle without touching the sides. Stack the circles so that the foil is in the center of the pile. Place the stack of paper on top the rack to protect the batik bundle from excess moisture. Make sure the paper does not touch the sides of the kettle.

1. Bring the water to a boil. Make sure the water level is below the rack and that it does not splash up onto the papers as it boils.

2. Center the bundle on top of the papers. Cover with the padded lid.

3. Steam for 2-4 hours checking the water level periodically. Never let the kettle boil dry. Be sure to set a loud kitchen timer as a reminder or place marbles or your lucky penny into the boiling water. The rattle of the marbles or penny will signal that there is water in the pot. When the sound level changes or stops, you will know it is time to add more boiling water.

When the steaming is completed remove the coil from the kettle and carefully unroll the batik. Hang it to dry or iron it out between pressing cloths while it is damp to create a smooth, soft hand to the fabric. The permanently colored fabric can now be washed or dry cleaned to remove the last traces of wax.

Photos by Nicolas Kane

1 Center coil on papers.

2 Cover with padded lid.

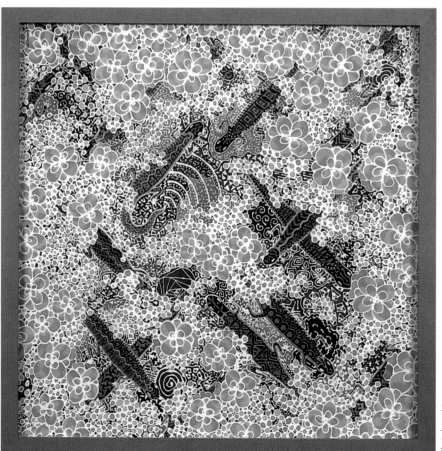

Newt Courtship
by Robin Paris,
33.5"w x 33.5"h.

Photo by artist

Nomad, by Kyrle Boardman, 23"w x 16"h.

Batik, machine embroidery, quilting with painted frame.

In Summary

Your batik is now wax-free and ready for the finishing touches and the final presentation. It can be reworked with new resist motifs, overdyed, patterned with discharged designs, or embellished with metallic paints, embroidery, appliqué, or other surface design materials. Garments, accessories, and home décor items can now be sewn and embellished.

If you are using the batik as part of a quilt, the completed design can be used as a single image or it can be cut into smaller sections and pieced together with other batiks and/or commercial fabrics to form entirely new design motifs. Remember that the quilt backings can also be decorated with resist art.

If you have created the batik as a fine art piece, it is ready to be stretched and framed, or mounted as a wall hanging, or draped in a 3-dimensional configuration. Paper batiks are usually matted or mounted behind glass while fabric batiks are often stretched over an opaque white fabric and framed without glass. Whatever presentation method you choose, your batik will reflect your unique artistry and accomplishment.

Above: *The Letter*
by Kay Baxandall,
21"w x 16"h.

Repetition of
rectangular shapes.

Left: *How Many Zebras?*
by Jill Walden,
16"w x 16"h.

Negative and positive
lines of varying widths.

directs the way in which the elements are used. The type of resist and the tools used for applying it to the fabric affect the characteristics of the shapes and lines. Colors and values are often planned with the overlapping succession of light to dark dyebaths in mind. Textures unique to batik are created through cracking, incising, erosion, and other waxing techniques, and space is often considered in terms of flat pattern on the picture plane rather than the illusion of depth and volume.

ART ELEMENTS

Shape, line, color, texture, value, and space are the building blocks of art. Even though these elements of art are universal, they are flexible enough to allow each artist to maintain a unique approach no matter the medium or content of his or her work. When we view a work of art, we might not always be overtly aware of the ways in which the artist utilized the elements but we do respond to the pleasing unity achieved through their skillful application.

SHAPE is the area within an enclosed boundary. In two-dimensional art, shape is flat; in three-dimensional art, it is volume. Shape is a natural outcome of batik's methods and materials. Areas of wax automatically form hard-edged shapes, as do the lines of wax used to wall-in selected sections of the design.

LINE is used to define the edge, or boundary, of a form. It is an abstraction, a contrivance not actually found in our three-dimensional world, but one that the artist uses to define shape, create texture, or depict the contour of a form. Line is also used to create movement and direction. The rhythmic repetition of lines creates the appearance of motion.

Design Considerations

Design is given order and structure through the skillful use of certain parameters called the *elements of art and the principles of design*. The art elements include shape, line, color, value, texture, and space. The principals of design govern the visual elements through the use of balance, harmony, contrast, rhythm, and

dominance. The basic *elements of art* and their governing *principles of design* are utilized by all artists and artisans regardless of their media.

Surface designers are no exception. The decorative patterns they create take shape through the skillful manipulation of the art elements and their governing design principles. Designers who work in batik find that the medium often

A series of shapes, colors, or the prominent contours of selected forms, can create invisible lines that guide the eye around the design.

Line is an important element of batik. Tjanting and brushes create expressive lines of wax in all widths, lengths, and configurations. Lines used to wall-in sections of the design in preparation for dyeing often become dominant elements of a finished motif.

COLOR directs the way in which we perceive a design and determines the psychological, social, and emotional content. The batik process challenges the artist with its unique demands of color usage. The dyeing methods affect the selection of the palette, the sequence in which the hues are applied, and the range and intensity of colors.

VALUE refers to the lightness or darkness of a color. Black, white, and shades of gray are actually considered values, not colors. High contrast describes the acute differences between light and dark while low contrast refers to subtle, closely related shades. Volume is revealed when value is used to define the light and shadows on a surface. The illusion of depth is created when the foreground objects are defined with high-contrasting values and receding objects with less discernable, low-contrasting shades. Emotional content is also revealed by value. Dark shades are often perceived as mysterious, dangerous, or sad while light shades are seen as happy, peaceful, and friendly.

Batik designers must plan the value as an integral part of the design. If immersion-dyeing techniques are used, the lightest colors are usually applied first followed by graduating values that work toward the final, darkest one.

TEXTURE is the tactile quality of a surface. There are *actual* textures that we can touch and feel and there are *simulated* textures — those created by the artist to give the visual appearance of texture. We "feel" the surfaces of simulated textures with our eyes, not our

Left: *Barn*
by Heather Gatt,
37cm x 47cm.

High contrasting values.

Below: *Untitled*
by Janet Lindsay,
36"w x 36"h.

Batik on silk textured with woven metallic strips.

Photo by Robert Groh

Resting Place
by Vikki Pignatelli,
87"w x 88"h.

Mixed media quilt utilizes
decorative space.

Photo by artist

The Kathi: Arrive, by Rosi Robinson,
56cm x 71cm.

Simulated space created through changes
in scale, value and intensity.

fingertips. Simulated surface textures can be invented, based on nothing more than the artist's imagination or they can be abstractions inspired by actual surfaces.

The *actual* texture of batik is the surface of the fabric on which it is created. This surface texture is usually not as important to the design as the *simulated* texture.

SPACE is an important part of surface design even when it is two-dimensional. Surface design utilizes space as a visual experience rather than an actual one and there are many different approaches and outcomes to its depiction. Simulated space gives the illusion of actual space through the use of perspective, changes in the scale and varying intensities and values. *Decorative space,* on the other hand, is solely the contrivance of the artist's imagination. Its main consideration is the two-dimensional plane on which the design elements are arranged. Decorative space can appear as flat-pattern or it can give the illusion of deep and infinite space through overlapping shapes, size and color changes.

Historically, batik was created as a flat-pattern surface decoration and many artists still favor this approach. Others prefer to create a more spatial look to their designs.

Whether they create flat-pattern designs or ones with the illusion of depth, batik artists must skillfully combine their knowledge of shape, line, color, value, and texture to convey the desired spatial effects they choose.

PRINCIPLES OF DESIGN

The elements of art are arranged using certain rules of organization called the *principles of design.* These principles give unity to the visual elements through the use of balance, harmony, contrast, rhythm, dominance, and subordination.

Above: *Cormorants on the Sandbank* by Anne Balogna, 41"w x 32"h.

Approximate symmetry.

Left: *Caplin,* by Diana Dabinett, 40"w x 64.5"h.

Controlled spacing and repetition of similar shapes create swirling motion.

BALANCE is the visual equilibrium that unites the various art elements into a cohesive whole. There is symmetrical balance and asymmetrical balance. Symmetrical balance divides the design along an imaginary axis and presents the two halves as mirror images of one another. This equal distribution of visual weight proves almost too static and predictable at times. To create greater visual interest, the artist sometimes makes minor changes so that the design is only approximately symmetrical.

Asymmetrical balance is more dynamic and challenging. Visual weight is distributed unevenly throughout the design yet the finished work still has a sense of cohesion and unity.

HARMONY provides cohesiveness within a design through the repetition of similar visual elements. Reoccurring shapes, lines, colors, values, and textures form a satisfying consistency and also act as guideposts that lead the eye through the design.

CONTRAST adds interest and focus through the use of dissimilar

Early Morning Wind
by Susan Schneider,
48"w x 34"h.

Rhythmic repetition
of shapes creates
the motion of the
wind-tossed laundry.

Neapolitan Night
by Muffy Clark Gill,
26"w x 18"h.

Combination of
contrasting and
close-value colors.

through the emphasis of a selected element as the motif's main center of interest. The other elements are used to support this focal point and are secondary to it. Repeated variations of the dominant visual elements guide the eye through the design.

SUBORDINATION of selected elements gives support to the design's main focus. It would be quite confusing if all elements had the same visual importance in a design. By making some elements less important, the artist creates clarity and provides the viewer a visual path through the work.

elements. A circle in a sea of squares appears far more vibrant that one placed in a grouping of like circles. Contrast gives a focal point and adds much needed highlights to a design.

RHYTHM is the sense of action or movement created through the controlled spacing and repetition of similar elements. This visual movement not only unifies the elements of the design, but also helps to set the emotional tone of the work, creating a cohesive overall point of view, or mood.

DOMINANCE creates unity

Batik designers, like all surface designers, apply the art elements and the governing principles of design using uniquely personal points of view. Their final designs take shape not only from the formal design considerations but also from the influence of past experiences and internal aesthetic responses. Batik's unique application and dyeing methods also effect the look of their finished designs. Some batik designers are influenced by historically significant designs and production methods of the past while others are inspired by less traditional resist methods.

The batik artists' skill in melding the formal design considerations, personal influences, and the many varied production methods assure a rich diversity of creative and original surface designs.

Clothing and Accessories

Javanese batik was developed chiefly as a method of clothing decoration. Quality and production methods varied from the exquisitely intricate hand waxed designs applied to royal and ceremonial garments to the mass-produced fabrics whose designs were applied with stamping tools called tjaps.

Eventually batik garments became so sought after that manufacturing industries and trade companies were established in Indonesia and other countries to make and export the clothing. Today batik clothing is still highly prized and garments created by a wide variety of production methods are found in galleries, boutiques, and craft bazaars throughout the world.

Dresses, jackets, coats, and shirts are often designed and the outlines of the pattern pieces copied onto the fabric before the wax and dyes are applied. Be sure

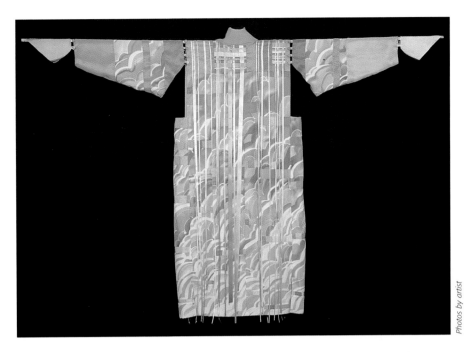

Photos by artist

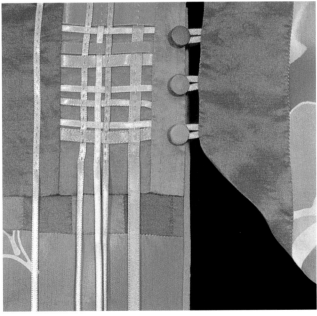

Cloud Coat
(back view & detail)
by Karen Perrine.

to leave a seam allowance when planning the register of the design. Details such as fasteners and linings can be made from additional batik fabrics.

Vests make ideal garments for batik embellishments. The flat, loose fitting construction of a vest provides an unfettered surface on which to apply the resist and dye.

The rich colors and fanciful patterns of batik designs make sophisticated wardrobe accents when applied to scarves, hats, and other accessory items. It is a challenge to design, sew, and embellish fashion accessories. If you need a jump-start for your beginning projects, pre-sewn clothing and accessories are available.

Silk Shantung Jacket
by Joyce Dewsbury.

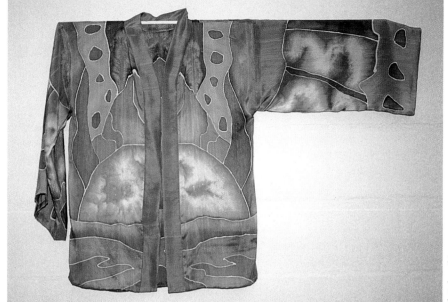

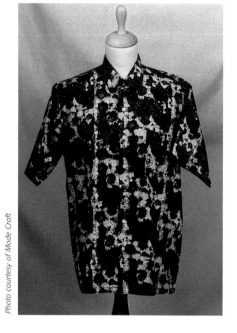

Man's Batik Shirt
Designed by Abdul Jalil Che Lah
for Mode Craft,
Kuala Lumpur, Malaysia.

Emu Hunting Vest
by Alison Hall.

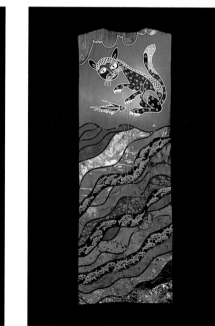

Cat Batik Duster (front & back)
by Giselle Gilson Blythe.

Left: *Padded Heart Box*
by Joyce Dewsbury,
4.5"h x 4"d.

Middle: *Batik Purses*
by Nancy King.

Left: *Jewelry*
by Nancy King.

Batik covered shapes
embellished with small charms.

Right: *Ceramic tile,* by Joanne Gigliotti.
Tjanting-applied wax and hand painted glazes on white ceramic tiles.

Below: *Wild Iris*
by Diana Dabinett, 72"w x 102"h.
Diptych wall hanging.

Right: *With Love and Apologies to Vincent*
by Nancy King, 24"w x 21"h.
Batiked, pieced, and machine quilted wall hanging.

Home Décor Items

Commercially produced batiks are popular as draperies, wall coverings, and upholstery textiles. Also in demand are the one-of-a-kind home décor items individually created from the more traditional methods and materials.

Wall hangings are a popular presentation format for batik designs. There are many finishing methods for batik hangings. They can be hemmed with a casing and hung with a dowel, or curtain rings can be attached along the top edge to accommodate a decorative rod.

They can also be sewn onto a fabric backing or stretched over frames.

Graphics, such as greeting cards, illustrations, and posters are marketed in both original and commercially printed forms.

Photo by John Robert Williams

Left: *As Forest Angels Gather*
by Terry Haugen, 13"w x 19"h.

Limited edition print from original batik.

Below Top: *Pelican Screen*
by Alison Hall, each panel 1.5m x 60cm.

Sectional batik on silk.

Below Bottom: *Folk Tunes in Flight*
by Sandra Grassi Nelipovich, 24"w x 30"h.

Batik illustration.

Photo by artist

Batik stretched on hoop
by Susan Schneider,
10" across.

Photo by artist

Above: *Batiked egg*
by Bernadette DiPietro.

Right: *Stones wrapped in batiked tissue paper*
by Christa Corner.

Above: *The Dream Weaver*
by Gretchen Lima, 24" tall.

Mixed media doll with commercial batik.

Ukrainian Easter eggs have been enjoyed for centuries. Elaborate wax designs are often applied with a needle embedded in a cork because the tjanting is too large and awkward for these tiny patterns.

Dolls make unique batik projects. The facial features can be waxed and dyed before the toy is sewn and stuffed or clothing and accessories can be created from commercial or batik fabrics.

In Summary

Surface design is a term that describes the patterns and motifs that embellish textiles. Batik, one of the oldest known surface design media, has been used since ancient times to decorate fabrics with intricate patterns and luminous colors. Successful designs, whether they are applied to clothing, accessories, or home-décor items utilize universal design criteria. The elements of art and the principles of design govern the formal structure of the batik design, serving to organize the many parts into a unified and cohesive whole. Of course batik artists and designers bring uniquely individual points of view to this formal structure, combining it with personal experience, interests, imagination, and technical skill to produce a rich variety of surface design.

Lexi, by Shelley Thornton,
24" tall.

Cloth doll with commercial
batik fabrics.

Within Your Reach (and detail)
by Julie Duschack, 39"w x 112"h.

Layered image incorporated batik,
hand painting, piecing, net overlays,
and machine stitching and beading.

Batik as Fine Art

What is art and what is craft? That was a hotly debated topic during my years as an art student. Art — fine art — was considered the erudite: craft the plebeian. It was assumed that fine art, by far the more important of the two, rose out of aesthetic idealism and self-expression. Craft was its less important handmaiden, there to serve a useful purpose or decorate a surface. To paraphrase Eliot's J. Alfred Prufrock, "...it was not prince Hamlet nor was meant to be."

The division between art and craft was still in place when I applied for a National Endowment grant in the category of painting — batik painting. I was contacted by the selection committee and asked that I allow them to transfer my application to the craft division because batik was a craft, not a fine art medium. No amount of reasoning or arguing could persuade them otherwise. I refused to allow the change because I believed emphatically that art should not be so narrowly defined and that batik was as valid a painting medium as oil paint, acrylic, or casein. In the end I did not qualify for consideration for the grant I so wanted.

Today this seems a stale and petty argument. Arbitrary lines of distinction have blurred as art and craft merge into a more inclusive whole. Of course there is craft in the

Winter Woods Installation
by Diana Dabinett, 100"w x 144"h.

Photo by Ned Pratt

creation of art and art in the making of craft. No longer is one defined strictly by media or the other by its purported usefulness. Craft can be as much for the sole purpose of aesthetics as it is for a more utilitarian intent and fine art is made from just about anything and everything imaginable; broken plates, rancid lard, old tires, and wax and dye. Batik has gone from a skilled craft to an eloquent fine art as artists from around the world explore the abundant possibilities of wax and dye, and

their outpouring makes it clear that batik can go beyond its technical limitations to become a diverse and significant means for self-expression.

The acceptance of batik as an expressive fine art medium is quite a departure from the early Javanese tradition in which it was considered a fabric embellishment, created through a collective effort using long-established design and production methods. Set motifs with rigid symbolism and color assignment were passed down from generation

Photo by Annmarie Kaiser

Photo by William Zinner

to generation. These motifs were drawn and waxed on traditionally prepared fabric by a large group of artisans. Another group dyed, cleaned, and color-set the fabric. Self-expression was subordinated to tradition, individual style yielded to established criterion, and the finished lengths of fabric bore no trace of the individual personalities who created them.

Now there are as many approaches to the batik process as there are artists who practice it. Each artist's vision is made manifest through an individual aesthetic response and a variety of inventive techniques. Batik has transcended its crafting tradition to become a medium capable of unique and powerful expression.

Portfolio

A work of art combines skill and inventiveness with materials and processes, established elements of design, rules of composition, and personal vision. This combination forms a work that is more than the sum of its parts. It creates a visual experience that can take us beyond the technical expertise to a universal truth. The work of art becomes a cognitive and emotional trigger, eliciting from within us a response of empathy that transcends time, place, and language.

The following examples show the range and depth that is possible when batik is used as a fine art medium.

Top: *Spectator II*
by Chuck Kaiser,
17"w x 11"h.

Left: *Layered Hillside*
by Eloise Piper,
40"w x 52"h.

THE LANDSCAPE TRADITION

"To him who in the love
of Nature holds
Communion with her visible
forms, she speaks
A various language."

– William Cullen Bryant

Whether it is the awesome beauty, majestic power, variations of place or season's changing mantle, landscape has long been a favored theme for artists. Urban landscapes as well as rural scenes capture the imagination of today's batik artist.

Landscape on My Mind
by Joyce Dewsbury,
46.5"w x 51"h.

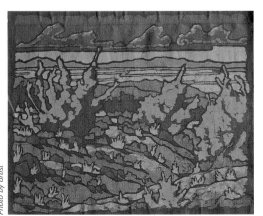

Top: *New York Skyline*
by Jill Walden,
50"w x 21"h.

Left: *Breathing Slowly*
by Stephanie Love,
19"w x 16"h.

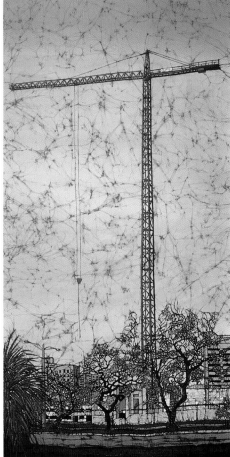

Top: *Amish Buggy*
by Terri Haugen,
34"w x 14"h.

Above: *Wedding Path*
by Marilyn Salomon,
24"w x 22"h.

Left: *Scroll Series*
by Arnelle Dow,
28"w x 22"h.

Right: *Above it All*
by Katherine Hicks Tsonas,
28"w x 54"h.

STILL-LIFE

"I firmly believe that if art speaks clearly about something relevant to people's lives, it can change the way they perceive reality."

– Judy Chicago

A culture's standards of beauty, social customs, and ethical values are reflected through the ordinary tools and artifacts of daily life. For over five hundred years artists have been recording arrangements of common objects to reveal the humble yet profound insights of who we are. The still life challenges the artist with its complexities of juxtaposing surface textures, colors, shapes, and spatial relationships.

Quite often the still life is used to showcase the artist's virtuosity. The delft hand of a master can transform puddles of dense and lifeless pigment into transparent glass, dewy flowers, and shimmering satin. The still life also has a long tradition as a teaching tool. Apples and armor make stalwart and unflinching models that will hold a pose for as long as the struggling apprentice finds necessary.

Rhododendrons by Elizabeth Sykes, 12"w x 18"h.

Right: *Still Life* by Kay Baxandall, 14"w x 18"h.

Below Left: *Zig Zag* by Muffy Clark Gill, 24"w x 36"h.

Below Right: *Perfume Bottles* by Arnelle Dow, 26"w x 22"h.

Right: *Islands From the Sky: Ridges and Rivers* by Mary Edna Fraser, 16' x 23'.

Below Top: *Islands From the Sky: Global Perception* by Mary Edna Fraser, 876 square feet.

Below Bottom: *Pathways Installation* by Diana Dabinett & Tara Bryan, 35' x 35' gallery space.

SITE-SPECIFIC ART

*"Locations and times —
what is it that meets them all,
Whenever and wherever,
and makes me at home?
Forms, colors, densities, odors —
what is it that corresponds
with them?"*

– Walt Whitman

Art that is created for an exact location is called site-specific art. These works are often commissioned by art grants, corporate, or government sponsorship. Examples are found in every age and every culture ranging from Egyptian tomb paintings, chapel ceilings in the Vatican, to the walls of many a United States post office. Constructivism, Installations, Environmental Art, Earthworks, Conceptual and Process Art, and Happenings are all part of the tradition of site-specific art.

The artists who create these works must meet the special challenge of combining personal creative vision with the restrictions of assigned size and space. Form must merge with function and imagery be matched to audience.

Left: *Bali Bubble*
by Linda Kaun, 19.5"w x 25.5"h.

Below: *Let's Pretend*
by Natalie Guess, 12"w x 15"h.

Bottom: *Papa*
by Lila Hahn, 26"w x 18"h.

PEOPLE

*"O wad some Pow'r
the giftie gie us
To see oursels as others see us!
It wad frae mony a blunder free
us, and foolish notion."*

– Robert Burns

Ever since an unknown Paleolithic artisan created the first amply endowed fertility goddess, the human image has been the single most popular subject for the artist. The figure has been portrayed in total and in detail, as young and old, male and female, nude, costumed, alone and in groupings. Images sometimes flatter, sometimes cajole, and sometimes hold a mirror to our darkest and innermost secrets. Whether enhancing or enlightening, our own likeness is a theme which both artist and audience never tire of, for it records our history, our values, and our truths, and states for all times and all peoples, "I am!"

Top: *Laine and Easton*
by Jessica Hughes,
30"w x 30"h.

Bottom: *Tennessee Williams*
by Susan Schneider,
24"w x 34"h.

Above: *Man With Pint*
by Ruth Holmes.

Graham and Sophie
by Jessica Hughes,
20"w x 16"h.

Curlew
by Anne Balogna,
20"w x 28"h.

PHOTO REALISM

*"A photograph is a secret
about a secret.
The more it tells you the
less you know."*

– Diane Arbus

Artwork was once the only means available to record the visual world. Rendered images of people, places, and events have left a record of the past that we often accept as fact even though it is filtered through each era's social, political, philosophic, and religious beliefs as well as each artist's personal interpretations and biases. It is sometimes difficult to realize that what we think of as realism is actually far more subjective than empirical because of this flux in attitudes and changing influences on personal expression.

During the later half of the nineteenth century, as a reaction to the contrived images of Neoclassicism and the excesses of Romanticism, some artists returned to Naturalism to capture the immediacy, or realness, of everyday life. A newly invented device, the camera, influenced their approach to this realism. Artists were not only challenged to render meticulously accurate images, but at the same time they now tried to reveal a deeper insight or truth — one that could not be captured through the lens of a camera. Real was becoming a personal, internal truth, one that went beyond the mere physical appearance.

More than a century later, artists' concepts of reality are still influenced by the camera. The Pop Art culture of the nineteen-sixties produced a realism that mirrored the technology of the photographic process and methods of commercial printing and advertising. Often called Super-realism, this genre emphasizes the random cropping and emotional detachment of the snapshot and has the appearance of darkroom production techniques such as half tones, over exposures, and value scales. Subject matter is sometimes enlarged far beyond its actual size, forcing the viewer to rethink their concept of reality.

Right: *Denali*
by Helen Carkin,
25.5"w x 21"h.

Below: *Girl With Ipu*
by Helen Carkin,
25.5"w x 21"h.

Left: *Puppies*
by Jessica Hughes,
30"w x 20"h.

Below: *Untitled*
by Jim Nordmeyer,
30"w x 12"h.

ABSTRACTION

Toward the end of the nineteenth century artists began looking beyond the illusion of reality created on the material surface to find a new reality, one that was based on internal truths rather than outer appearances. The Cubists broke the image into sphere, cube, and cone. Futurists, influenced by the horrors of war and the industrial society's inequities, reflected the violence and strife through fractured images of motion. Dadaists gave us art of the absurd to show the cynicism and nihilism of a war-torn world, and the Surrealists created dream-like images influenced by Freud's psychoanalytical explorations into the subconscious.

Abstractionists of the early twentieth century explored the emotional content of recognizable subject matter while the Non-objectivists attempted to remove all traces of recognizable references from their images. By mid-century, some Abstract Expressionists were exploring ways to express emotional content through vigorous action, basing their reality on the actual making of the art, not the final result. Painters also began to explore the purity of the elements of color, line, and shape through analytical and geometric patterns that were devoid of all emotional content and recognizable subject matter.

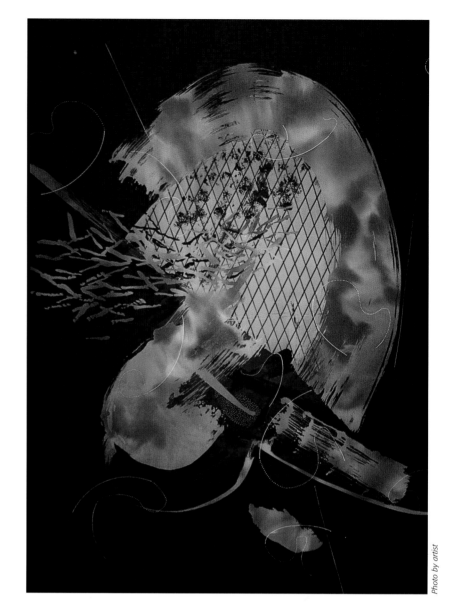

Photo by artist

Photo by artist

Above: *Release*
by Noel Dyrenforth,
94cm x 127cm.

Left: *Fly Away Home*
by Ginny Lohr,
40"w x 44"h.

Tapestry
by Annie Phillips,
18"w x 30"h.

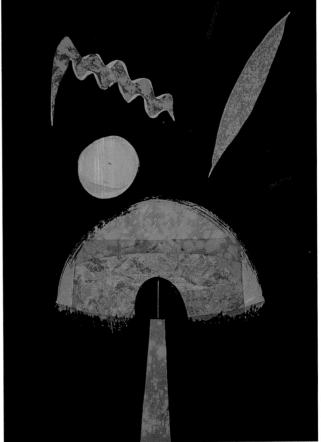

Above: *They Should Have Been Flowers*
by Joyce Dewsbury, 40.5"w x 41"h.

Below: *Affirm,* by Noel Dyrenforth, 94cm x 127cm.

In Summary

There are as many approaches to the medium of batik as there are artists who practice it. Each artist's unique vision is created through the combination of the formal elements of design, a variety of inventive techniques, and a personal aesthetic response. The diverse outpouring of images proves that batik is certainly a personal and richly expressive fine art as well as an exacting craft.

Batik in Quilting

The word quilt *once conjured up the image of great-grandma's feather bed made cozy with comforters pieced from the family's cast-off garments — here, a patch from Pa's worn out serge suit, there a patch of brother's red flannel work shirt. Yesteryear's quilter might not have known that quilting dated back over 500 years, or that it was once used to fashion armor, warm clothing, and decorative linens as well as bedding, but she did know the importance of thrift and the satisfaction of a creative, yet practical, endeavor.*

And so traditional designs such as Log Cabin, Wedding Ring, Tumbling Blocks, Lone Star, and the random Crazy Quilt were cut and tediously pieced together during the fragments of time between cooking and cleaning and child rearing. Aside from the handful of barracked or convalescing soldiers and prisoners of war who fashioned quilts from bits and pieces of worn uniforms, quiltmaking was a craft mostly practiced by the anonymous and industrious woman; blankets were the practical and well-used result of her efforts to waste not, want not.

Today the word brings to mind a vastly different image. Along with the traditionally patterned comforters, we now picture sophisticated, one-of-a-kind wall hangings sewn from an expansive array of commer-

Twilight Trees, by Susan Stein, 61"w x 61"h.
Commercial batiks and hand dyed fabrics, machine pieced.

cial and hand decorated fabrics and embellished with notions and a variety of painting and crafting techniques. No longer anonymous, today's quilter is artist, designer, and master sewer, and her work is just as

likely to be found at an international quilt exhibition as it is on a feather bed. Quilting is no longer the exclusive domain of the thrifty housewife and occasional soldier. Formally trained artists and textile designers

Left: *Dreamweavers*
by Ricky Tims.

Purchased batik panel with improvisational "caveman" pieced and quilted border.

Above: *Pond Reflections at Dawn*
by Vikki Pignatelli,
76"w x 81"h.

Commercial batiks and overdyed fabrics, machine pieced and quilted.

as well as self-taught crafters find it to be an expressive and flexible medium; one that can be taken far beyond the tradition of blanket making to an inventive merging of art and craft.

The most innovative change in recent quiltmaking is the use of embellishment techniques to alter the fabrics, personalizing them to suit the creative vision of the quilt-artist. Batik, gutta, overdyeing, and discharge dyeing are the most common methods used to customize the fabric surface. Sometimes used alone or in combination with one another, these techniques bring a new approach to the design and construction of quilt art. The quilt is now a canvas whose imagery is as varied and ingenious as the artists who call themselves quiltmakers.

Origins of Quiltmaking

Before reviewing the various resist fabrics used by the quiltmaker let me give a brief explanation of quilting and a word about its origins. A quilt consists of three layers: padding (called wadding or batting) sandwiched between two pieces of fabric and held in place with stitching or tufting. The craft was developed over five hundred years ago in the cold, northern climates of both Europe and Asia. It is often thought that quilt art was exclusively used to fashion comforters, but it was most probably applied to decorative items and articles of clothing long before it evolved into the warm bedding we think of today. One or both sides of the quilt were of solid-

colored cloth or were decorated with embroidery, appliqué, or woven designs. The development of printed textiles led to the use of colorful printed fabrics in quilting. By the mid 1700s blankets with the familiar pieced designs came into popularity in both Europe and America.

The actual *quilting* is the top-stitching that secures the wadding and the fabrics together. The term *quilting* also refers to the task of applying the stitching. For centuries intricate designs made up of thousands of tiny, evenly spaced stitches were laboriously sewn by hand. It took time, patience, and nimble fingers to produce these all-over quilted patterns. At times, much like the intricate waxing process of batik, it was handiwork

Juxtaposition (and detail)
by Giselle Gilson Blythe,
50"w x 63"h.

Original batik, hand painted and
overdyed fabrics, machine pieced
and quilted.

Photos by David Blythe

for and by the leisure-class woman. As its popularity among the wealthy dwindled, quilting was embraced as a useful blanket-making craft for the ordinary woman. The tedious job of topstitching the surface of a pieced blanket often became a group activity for hardworking housewives who occasionally gathered together to stitch and socialize.

By the early 20th century mass production of affordable bedding, a shift in woman's place from home to the workforce, and a devaluation of handcraft brought a decline in quilting. Except for a short revival sparked by need during the Great Depression, it remained a quaint but little practiced pastime until the late 1960's when a resurgence of home crafting activities brought quilting back from the brink of extinction. Since then it has evolved into the sophisticated and widely practiced art form we see today.

Quiltmaking Today

The quilt artist now has at his/her disposal a dazzling variety of equipment, fabrics, notions and techniques. Inventive uses of new technologies also play a roll in the making of quilts. The camera, projector, copy machine, and computer have certainly influenced the ways in which designs are generated. Computerized sewing machines and customized quilting appliances have

The Paper Doll Quilt (and details) by Rebekka Seigel, 64"w x 63"h.

Photo transfer of a 1950's paper doll. Garments are small, removable quilts that attach to the doll with Velcro. Outlines of the clothing are batiked onto the wardrobe pages to assure that the garments will be put back in their proper places.

Photos by Greg Seigel

altered the methods used to join and secure the fabrics. A modern quilt is as likely to be topstitched with elaborate machine-quilted designs as with hand sewn motifs.

And of course there is the fabric! Quilters can now choose from hundreds upon hundreds of exquisite textiles and a huge assortment of yarn, thread, ribbon, fringe, braid, and binding. Also available are all types of novelties and notions such as wire mesh, Mylar, metallic fibers, buttons, beads, and pressed-metal and plastic charms.

Portfolio

Of all the many changes in quilt-making one of the most pronounced is the manipulation of the fabric surface with various embellishment techniques. Designs that incorporate batik, gutta, overdyeing, and discharge dyeing can be found in every major exhibition of contemporary quilts. Here are some examples that show the personal and innovative imagery that is possible when batik is used in quilting.

ORIGINAL BATIK

"Without this playing with fantasy no creative work has ever yet come to birth. The debt we owe to the play of imagination is incalculable."

– Carl Gustav Jung

The response to the tactile experience that delights the batik artist also captivates the quilt artist. The kinesthetic pleasure found in the flow of the wax and in the metamorphosis of the fabric as it is dyed is also found in the manipulation of fabric, needle and thread. Maybe that is one of the reasons that quiltmakers often use batik to personalize their quilt imagery. Both quilt and batik artists speak of losing themselves in their work. Time and place often give way to a meditative state in which all awareness is focused on the creative process.

There is an immense sense of achievement and personal growth when we get in touch with the wellspring of creativity that is within us. We are all endowed with abundant creativity that is just waiting to gain expression. The challenge of designing and producing original imagery will help you to expand your creative potential. What better way to exercise this inner resource than to create original batik for your quiltmaking activities?

Photos by artist

Above: *Poppies* (and detail) by Gilda Baron, 20"w x 16"h.

Hand and machine embroidery on original batik.

Left: *Great Mother of Her Serpents* by Rebekka Seigal, 61"w x 69"h.

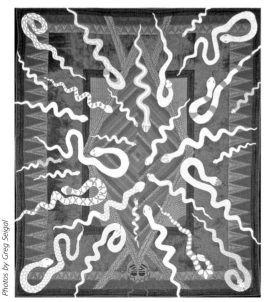

Photos by Greg Seigal

Photo by David Combes

Hundred Acres by Sheila Cook, 56"w x 70"h.

PURCHASED BATIK ITEMS

"Things must be right in themselves and good for use."
– Eric Gill

You may want to use batik in your quilt designs but the mere thought of the time and effort it will take to custom-make the fabric keeps you from doing so. You will be happily surprised at how many sources there are for wonderful readymade batik items. If you are lucky enough to have traveled to Indonesia, Hawaii, India, Africa or some other country which produces batik, you might have brought home a length of batik fabric — or maybe a garment or two.

Even without foreign travel you will find many sources for batik. Specialty clothing shops and boutiques carry batik clothing. Batik-patterned tablecloths, napkins, and bedspreads can be found in home décor shops or houseware departments.

Check out your local thrift store as a resource for batik fabrics. I have found a wide assortment of batik in men's shirts, bathing trunks, ladies dresses, scarves, and blouses.

Thrift Store blouse.

Photos by Bernice Meissner

Thrift Store bathrobe (detail).

COMMERCIAL BATIK FABRICS

*"Things are not done beautifully.
The beauty is an integral part
of their being done."*

– Robert Henri

Commercially produced batik fabrics can be found in most quilt supply shops. These vary from the commercially printed fabrics that have the look of batik to actual resist patterns created by traditional production methods. Colors derived from modern chemical-based dyes are often reflective of the natural-dye colors that were used centuries ago. Many of these fabrics have the familiar veining and crazing.

To tell whether a fabric is real batik or a commercially printed facsimile check the back of the fabric. Printed patterns will have a right side and a wrong side while real batik will look the same on both sides of the cloth.

Quilters find that commercial fabrics add a richness and depth to their work and the batik designs create a distinctive contrast to the small-scale calico designs and solids of the more traditional quilting fabrics.

Top Left: *Sunrise – Ocean Isle*
by Ann Harwell,
54"w x 54"h.

Fabrics include commercial
batik, machine pieced
and quilted.

Bottom Left: *Basket Weave*
by Cathy Miranker,
41"w x 41"h.

Above: *African Rhythms*
by Lauren Rosenblum,
60"w x 90"h.

OVERDYEING

*"Change is one thing,
progress is another."*

– Betrand Russell

Overdyed fabrics are immensely popular with quilters. At quilt shows you will find that the majority of vendors sell bundles of fat quarters of overdyed solids and calicos. One can find fabrics that have been dyed evenly and ones that are mottled from having been twisted, tied, or scrunched during the dyeing process. Some fabrics have been splashed with more than one color for a hand painted look while others have been dyed multiple times or combined with discharge dyeing. Also popular are the bundles of four or five pieces of the same fabric each of which has been overdyed with gradating shades and tints of the same hue.

Overdyeing allows the quilter to use the exact colors and shades of fabric envisioned for each project. One fabric motif can be used for many different elements within the same design when it is overdyed with a variety of contrasting hues. Fabrics with dissimilar motifs or designs of vastly differing scale are made harmonious when they are overdyed with similar colors.

Experiment with various methods of applying the dye to the fabric and don't worry about the results. There is no right or wrong way to customize the color of the fabric, and the more experimental you are the more unique your fabrics will be.

Still Water, by Karen Perrine,
62"w x 100"h.

Batik, hand painted and overdyed fabrics, machine pieced and quilted.

Photo by artist

Photo by Dennis Le Croissette

Above: *Bonne Journée, M. Eiffel*
by Jill Le Croissette, 35"w x 31"h.

Commercial and overdyed batik, machine pieced.

Right: *The Length of Time's Uncertain Wing*
by Roxana Bartlett, 76"w x 76"h.

Hand painted and overdyed fabrics.

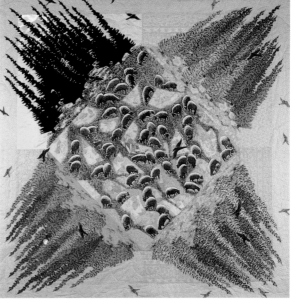

Photo by Ken Sanville

DISCHARGE-DYEING

*"It is a poor sort of memory
that only works backwards"
the Queen remarked.*

– Lewis Carroll

Commercial bleaching paste or a solution of chlorine bleach and water is used to remove the dye from areas of colored fabric. The lightened sections of fabric can be used as design elements or redyed with other hues. Quilters use discharge dyeing to customize traditional quilt fabrics and to alter hand painted, and overdyed surfaces. It is often used with batik to create combinations of colors that are not possible with traditional overlapping dyebaths. For instance bright green elements can be added to a bright red design if the designated areas are discharged of their color and the remaining red areas sealed with resist before the green dye is added.

Discharge paste can be applied to fabrics of varying weights and naps. Use it on woven stripes and plaids, printed patterns, solid colors, or on special discharge fabrics that have been pre-dyed with fugitive, easy-to-remove color.

Circling Autumn
by Jill Le Croissette,
40"w x 40"h.

Commercial batiks, hand dyed and discharged cottons, machine pieced and appliquéd, machine and hand quilted.

Above Right: *Midnight in the Garden of My Heart*
by Elizabeth Palmer Spilker,
33"w x 33"h.

Batik and discharged fabric, machine pieced.

Right: *Black Batik*
by Jan Smiley,
22"w x 24"h.

Wax resist on black discharge fabric.

Right: *Spring Maples*
by Lydia Johnston,
38"w x 19"h.

Original batiks and
overdyed fabrics,
machine pieced.

Upstream
by Elizabeth
Palmer Spilker,
33"w x 33"h.

Batik and hand painted
fabrics, machine pieced.

FRONT ART

*"The artist is faced with an
immense and desert sea,
…sans mâts, sans mâts,
ni fertiles îlots, and the mirror
he holds up to it is no bigger
than his own heart."*

– Jacques Maritain

A major change in quiltmaking over the past fifty years is in the surface imagery. It has gone from traditional geometric patterns and the occasional story-telling pictures, to highly personalized visual expressions.

There is no limit or restriction to the visual content of quilt art. Subject matter now includes any topic you can imagine. While attending a recent quilt show I was struck by the diversity of images and ideas. Ecology, conservation, breast cancer recovery, dreams, genealogy, gardening, religion, and vacation travels are just a few of the themes that were on display. This shift in imagery from traditional patterns to personal visions has been a major factor in the elevation of quilt from useful craft to expressive art.

BACK ART

"The artist serves humanity by feeding its hungry spirit..."
– Sylvia Shaw Judson

Back art has become an important part of the quilt, and many works are now exhibited in such a way as to show both front and back at the same time. The solid, nondescript quilt backings of yesterday have been replaced by carefully designed and executed works of art. Some quilt artists use similar motifs and methods to carry out a recurring theme on both sides of the quilt. Others create contrasting images by using very different materials, techniques and quilting patterns.

The quilt back can be embellished with wax or gutta resist, discharge dyeing, or hand painting in contrast to a pieced and quilted front design. Photo transfers, calligraphy, and stenciling techniques are also used to create unusual back art.

Photos by artist

Seeking Balance
by Linda Kaun,
29"w x 22"h x 4".

Cotton batik, machine quilted.

Left: *Under the Boardwalk*
(front and back details)
by Nancy King.

Batik and overdyed fabric, machine pieced and quilted.

MIXED MEDIA

"Variety is sweet in all things."
– Euripides

Mixed media is a term that is often used to describe quilt art. No longer is the design limited to a single method of construction. It is now commonplace to find quilts that are created through a combination of many different materials and processes. In fact, quilts often include so many different methods that it is sometimes hard to tell just how the image is derived. There are many needle art techniques to choose from. These can be combined with the manipulative techniques such as drawing, painting, wax resist, gutta resist, overdyeing, discharge dyeing, tie dyeing, photo transfer, block printing, silk screening, and mono printing.

Why not try mixing and matching a variety of materials and techniques on your next quilt project? Study the work of others to see successful combinations of techniques, or enroll in a workshop to learn a new method or two. Many of the materials and processes used by painters and graphic artists can be adapted to quiltmaking so don't overlook art classes as a means to stimulate new ideas. Sometimes just browsing the craft store or notions department is all it takes to spark your imagination. Unusual beads or buttons, interesting wooden charms, or some glittering metallic thread might be just the thing to inspire a stunning mixed media design.

Photo by artist

Barbie's Mexican Holiday
(and detail)
by Giselle Gilson Blythe,
31"w x 24"h.

Commercial batiks and overdyed
fabrics, machine pieced, hand tufted
and embellished with notions.

In Summary

Manipulation of the fabric surface
combined with the amazing ingenu-
ity and skill of the quilt artist has
helped to elevate quilting from the
bed to the boardroom wall. Quiltmakers have added many different
sewing and embellishment processes to their traditional quilting techniques. The unique and original imagery that emerges from these non-
traditional techniques often express-
es the social, emotional, and philosophic views of its creator. Back art is
an integral part of the quilt design
and often becomes a work of art
in its own right. Combinations of
materials and processes also play an
important role in quilt imagery.
Today's quiltmaking has merged
sewing craft with surface design and
fine art, and the exciting result is
now a highly regarded and much
collected art form.

Extemporary
by Christa Corner,
38cm x 25cm.

Batik with metallic leaf and
machine embroidery.

Conclusion

Batik is a unique and rewarding art form. I hope this book sparks your interest and encourages you to try your hand at it. As with any new skill, it takes time to become practiced and confident — time before your designs begin to flow effortlessly, time before you can skillfully handle wax and dye. If the results of your first efforts are not what you had planned, don't despair. Eventually, if you keep at it, you will find an easy outpouring of ideas and a smooth transition from ideas to images.

When I exhibit my batik paintings I am often asked how I develop the imagery. The answer is quite simple. I first "see" the complete image in my mind. I do not sketch ahead of time, but I do a lot of looking. Everywhere I go I collect bits and pieces of imagery that eventually make their way into the batiks. A lonely flophouse window from a nighttime Greyhound trip became a series of naked silhouettes on dim-lit window shades. Queen Anne's lace, snow-dusted stubbles of wheat, and the spring's first crocuses became part of the countless meadow paintings. Wet cobblestone streets, the neighbor's dog, my children at the playground — all the fragments of day-to-day life — seemed to effortlessly weave together to create these mind's-eye pictures.

Window, by Eloise Piper, 14"w x 16"h.

I do not draw on the silk for fear of damaging the delicate fabric. If the image in my mind is strong I can "see" not only the completed picture, but also each of the many individual layers of wax and color

Lily Pad Pond
by Eloise Piper,
42"w x 48"h.

that make up the finished design. I begin waxing on white silk, and whether there are five or thirty-five layers of color, I wax and dye what I "see" in sequence from the lightest hue to the darkest.

Other batik artists have their own unique methods for generating designs and transferring them to fabric. The radiant portraits by Jessica Hughes are meticulously planned. A photograph is the initial inspiration. A pencil drawing is made from the photograph to determine the value scale. The outline of the drawing is then transferred onto the fabric and the image is waxed and dyed. The palette of colors is not selected ahead of time. Instead, the various shades of gray are intuitively translated into color as the piece progresses. Even with the many steps that are used to arrive at the final image, the work has a fresh spontaneity because of the artist's skill and assuredness.

The powerful *Islands From the Sky* landscapes by Mary Edna Fraser are inspired by aerial views of the sinewy South Carolina coastal waters as seen from her family's 1946 four-cylinder silver Ercoupe. Both artist and pilot review maps to determine a flight plan based on the desired images. Once airborne, Mary Edna leans out the plane's open window to photograph the view below. Back in the studio she carefully

reviews the slides and often creates watercolor sketches of the selected images to establish the palette. If the work is to be a complex installation, a scale model is also built before the silk is waxed and dyed. Hundreds of hours go into the planning, design and execution of these remarkable batiks.

There is no definitive way of finding inspiration and no right or wrong way of turning that inspiration into art. Your process will be

different from mine, or any other artist's. A blend of life experience, knowledge, vision, and individual preference culminates in a personal form of expression for each of us. We need only to be open to the infinite possibilities of our creativity to develop our own imagery. Once you begin to transform inspiration into visual expression you will find that you have so many ideas that it will sometimes be hard to choose which one to pursue. You need not work at

Waiting
by Eloise Piper,
16"w x 18"h.

Photo by William Zinner

developing a particular style for true style is character, which is inherent in all that we are and all that we do.

I am also asked repeatedly how I manage to stay focused during the long and tedious process of waxing and dyeing the fabric. Surprisingly, this has never been a problem, even when a work has taken almost a year to complete. Many of the artists with whom I have spoken during the course of writing this book tell me the same thing. Different as the design process is for each of us, we all share a similar experience in the actual process of waxing and dyeing batik.

As one focuses on applying the wax, there develops an intense connection to the process — a feeling of being completely centered. It is almost as if you become one with the process. Some artists speak of this as a meditative state in which the passage of time seems irrelevant. Others refer to it as a spiritual experience. At one time or other we have all had the surprise of looking up from our work to discover that many hours have passed in what seemed like minutes. I hope that as you become confident with the batik process, you too experience this engrossing connection to your work.

To be completely absorbed in the creative process is indeed a profound and empowering experience.

I also hope that you have enjoyed looking at the diverse examples of batik that are included in this book. Many talented artists have contributed to this project and their work has been a constant source of amazement and delight to me. May you experience that same delight and let it be the impetus for your own explorations into the timeless and fascinating art of batik.

Eloise Piper
January, 2000

Suggested Reading

History

Prehistoric Art
Thomas G. Powell
Praeger New York 1966

A History of Dyed Textile
Stuart Robinson
MIT Press, Cambridge Mass. 1969

The Story of Craft
Edward Lucie-Smith
Cornell University Press 1981

**Ornament:
A Social History Since 1450**
Michael Snadin
Yale University Press 1996

**Indigo Textiles,
Technique and History**
Gösta Sandberg
Lark Books 1989

Textile Printing
Joyce Storey
Van Norstrand Reinhold
Company 1974

Fairy Fancy on Fabrics
Erwin Bindewald and Karl Kasper
Georg Westermann Verlag,
Braunschweig, Germany 1951

Woman in the Wall, by Sara Austin, 21" tall.
Direct dyeing, discharge dyeing and overdyeing with embroidery and beading.

Batik

Batik and Tie Dye Techniques
Nancy Belfer
Dover Publications, Inc
New York 1972

Batik Design
Pepin Van Roojen
Shambhala Publications, Inc 1997

**Batik, Tie Dye, Stenciling,
Silk Screen, Block Printing:
The Hand Decoration of Fabrics**
Francis J. Kafka
Dover Publications, Inc
New York 1959

Batik with Noel Dyrenforth
John Houston
Bobbs-Merrill
Indianapolis-New York 1975

The Technique of Batik
Noel Dyrenforth
B.T. Batsford Ltd. 1998

**Textile Dyeing and
Printing Simplified**
Nora Proud
Arco Publishing Company, Inc
New York 1974

Color

Color Magic for Quilters
Ann Seely and Joyce Stewart
Rodale Press, Inc 1997

Exploring Color
Nita Leland
North Light Publishers 1985

Color: The Quilter's Guide
Christine Barnes
That Patchwork Place, Inc
Bothell, WA

The Fabric Decoration Book
Patricia Ellisor Gaines
William Morrow & Company, Inc
New York 1975

**Hand Block Printing
and Resist Dyeing**
Susan Bosence
Arco Publishing Company, Inc
New York 1985

Design

Discovering Design
Marion Downer
Lothrop, Lee and Shepard
Company 1947

Imagery on Fabric
Jean Ray Laury
C & T Publishing, Inc 1997

Printed Textile Design
Terence Conran
The Studio Publications 1957

Quilting

The Essential Quilter
Barbara Chainey
David and Charles 1993

**The Complete Book
of Quiltmaking**
Michele Walker
Alfred A. Knopf, Inc. 1986

Quilting the World Over
Willow Ann Soltow
Chilton Book Company 1991

**A Painters Approach
to Quilt Design**
Velda Newman with
Christine Barnes
Fiber Studio Press 1996

Transforming Fabric
Carolyn Dahl
American Quilter's Society 1997

Natural dyes

Dye Plants and Dyeing
A handbook from the
Brooklyn Botanic Garden 1964

**Natural Colors;
Dyes From Plants**
Ida Grae
Macmillan Publishers Co. Inc.
1974

Natural Dyes
Sallie Pease Kierstead
Bruce Humphries, Inc. 1950

Vegetable Dyeing
Alma Lesch
Watson-Guptill Publications 1970

**Natural Dyes,
Plants and Processes**
Jack Kramer
Charles Scribner's Sons 1972

Chemical dyes

Dyeing to Quilt
Joyce Morri and Cynthia Myerberg
The Quilt Digest Press 1997

**Dyes and Paints: A Hands-on
Guide to Coloring Fabric**
Elin Noble
Fiber Studio Press 1998

Fabric Painting and Dyeing
David Green
Charles T. Branford Company 1972

**The Complete Book
of Fabric Painting**
Linda S. Kanzinger
The Alcott Press 1986

The Best of Silk Painting
Diane Tuckman and Jan Janas
North Light Books Cincinnati
Ohio 1997

**Silk Painting: The Artist's
Guide to Gutta and Wax
Resist Techniques**
Susan Louise Moyer
Watson-Guptill Publications 1991

**Silk Painting for Fashion
and Fine Art**
Susan Louise Moye
Watson-Guptill Publications 1995

Fabric Painting
Miranda Innes
A D K Publishing Book
Collins and Brown Limited 1996

Acknowledgements

Many thanks to all the people who participated in this project

Katie Kazan; Hand Books Press

Janet and Don Traynor; Design Books International

Steve Bridges; Bridges Design, Rockport, Massachusetts

Laura Couallier; Laura Herrmann Design, Maitland, Florida

Donald Miller; Art Critic, Pittsburgh Post Gazette

John E. Woods; San Diego, Californa

Alan Tisdale; San Diego, California

Bernice Meissner; Photographer, San Diego, California

Edward Kessler; Photographer, Carlsbad, California

Nicolas Kane; Photographer, San Diego, California

James David Hattin; Hattin Designs, Sacramento California

Khairuddin Mokhtar; Director, Mode Crafts SDN BHD, Kuala Lumpur, Malaysia

Martin Schweiger; Yorkshire, UK

Rita Trefois; Director of International Batik Gathering, Now & Again, Gent, Belgium

Sandie McCann and Kathy Engle; Hoffman California Fabrics, Mission Viejo, California

Becca DePue; Carlsbad, California

Dye Consultants

Bernice Colman; Fiber Arts Department, California State University at Northridge

Christa Corner, Lee Creswell, Becca DePue, dmotoko, Katherine Drew Dilworth

Mary Edna Fraser, Muffy Clark Gill, Sandra Holley, Linda Kaun, Farzaneh Samie Khosroshahi, Robin Paris

Companies

Bali Fabrications; West Sonoma, California

Batiks Etcetera; Fort Mill, South Carolina

Dharma Trading Company; San Rafael, California

Hoffman California Fabrics; Mission Viejo, California

Mode Crafts SDN BHD; Kuala Lumpur, Malaysia

Rupert, Gibbons and Spider; Healdsburg, California

PRO Chemical and Dyes, Somerset Massachusetts

Salsa Fabric Company, Silver Springs, Nevada

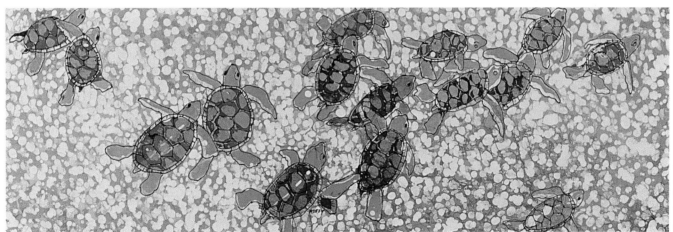

Turtle Beach, by Muffy Clark Gill, 30"w x 14"h.

Photo by Eric Strachan

Participating Artists

Sara Austin
Palos Verdes Peninsula, California, USA

Gilda Baron Harrow, England

Roxana Bartlett
Boulder, Colorado, USA

Kay Baxandall London, England

Giselle Gilson Blythe
Seattle, Washington, USA

Kyrle Boardman
Ashfield, Herefordshire, England

Anne Bologna Harbor View, Erie

Tara Bryan
Flatrock, Newfoundland, Canada

Helen Carkin Chico, California, USA

Sheila Cook Kent, England

Christa Corner Kent, England

Lee Creswell Cambridge, England

Jill Le Croissette
Carlsbad, California, USA

Diana Dabinett
St. John's, Newfoundland, Canada

Joyce Dewsbury
Gainesville, Florida, USA

Bernadette DiPietro
Ojai, California, USA

Katherine Drew Dilworth
Woodbine, Maryland, USA

dmotoko
Nishinomiya City, Hyogo, Japan

Marie Dorr Encinitas, California, USA

Arnelle Dow Cincinnati, Ohio, USA

Julie Duschack
Denmark, Wisconsin, USA

Noel Dyrenforth London, England

Kathy Engle
Mission Viejo, California, USA

Mary Edna Fraser
Charleston, South Carolina, USA

Linda Gass Los Altos, California, USA

Heather Gatt
North Yorkshire, England

Joanne Gigliotti
Gaithersburg, Maryland, USA

Muffy Clark Gill Naples, Florida, USA

Natalie Guess Naples, Florida, USA

Gono Unnayan Prochesta artists
Dhaka, Bangladesh

Lila Hahn Yuma, Colorado, USA

Alison Hall
Ceredigion, Whales, England

Ann Harwell
Wendell, North Carolina, USA

Terri Haugen
Frankfort, Michigan, USA

Donna Hickman
San Diego, California, USA

Sandra Holley
San Diego, California, USA

Ruth Holmes
Innishannon, County Cork, Erie

Jessica Hughes
Scwickley, Pennsylvania, USA

Cherry Jackson Melbourne, Australia

Lydia Johnston
North Pownal, Vermont, USA

Chuck Kaiser
Lancaster, Pennsylvania, USA

Linda Kaun
Yogyakarta, Java, Indonesia

Nancy King
Culver City, California, USA

Abdul Jalil Che Lah
Kuala Lumpur, Malaysia

Gretchen Lima
Sheboygan, Wisconsin, USA

Janet Lindsay
State College, Pennsylvania, USA

Ginny Lohr Getzville, New York, USA

Stephanie Love
Riverside, California, USA

Sandie McCann
San Clemente, California, USA

Bernice Meissner
San Diego, California, USA

Cathy Miranker
San Francisco, California, USA

Sandra Grassi Nelipovich
Anaheim, California, USA

Riki Kölbl Nelson
Northfield, Minnesota, USA

Jim Nordmeyer (deceased)

Robin Paris Cornwall, England

Karen Perrine
Tacoma, Washington, USA

Annie Phillips London, England

Vikki Pignatelli
Reynoldsburg, Ohio, USA

Rosi Robinson East Sussex, England

Lauren Rosenblum
Forest Hills, New York, USA

Linda M. Scholten Oxford, Ohio, USA

Susan Schneider London, England

Rebekka Seigel
Owenton, Kentucky, USA

Jan Smiley
Ft. Mill, South Carolina, USA

Marilyn Salomon
Thousand Oaks, California, USA

Elizabeth Palmer Spilker
Dublin, Ohio, USA

Susan Stein Delaware, Ohio, USA

Elizabeth Sykes Argyll, Scotland

Shelley Thornton
Lincoln, Nebraska, USA

Ricky Tims Arvada, Colorado, USA

Katherine Hicks Tsonas
Bryson City, North Carolina, USA

Jill Walden Cambridge, England

Rosanna Lynne Welter
West Valley City, Utah, USA

Cecile Yadro Moine, France

Thanks also to:

Gillian Christine Baker
Durham, United Kingdom

Sue Cowell Surrey, England

Becca DePue
Carlsbad, California, USA

Elena Koulik Moscow, Russia

Chetna Mehta
Chatsworth, California, USA

Dian Moore
Hummelstown, Pennsylvania, USA

Jeannie Rigby
Anderson, California, USA

Elizabeth Tamiso
East Berlin, Connecticut, USA

Index

Abstraction in batik 122-123
Activator 27, 75, 77
Additive color 44-45
Art elements 100-102

Bees' wax 13, 23-24
Brushes 21-22, 31-32

Calgon 27, 75, 82, 88
Calsolene oil 27, 74-75, 76, 78
Color arrangements 50-54
Color distribution 56
Color schemes, *see color arrangements*
Color temperature 50
Color wheel 46
Contrast 49, 103

Design principles 102-105
Direct dyeing 82
Discharge dyeing 87-88, 132
Discharge paste 25, 87-88
Dots 38-40
Dyes 27
  acid 68-73
  aniline 61
  chemical 61-62
  fiber-reactive 74-78
  natural 59-60, 64-67

Fabric 25-26
Fixer, *see activator*
Frames 21

Guttas 24-25

Hue 47-48, 51-53, 86

Immersion dyeing 76-79
Incising tools 42

La Foret, by Cecile Yadro, 32"w x 43"h.

Photo by artist

Intensity 48-49

Landscape in batik 114-115
Lines 32-33, 35-37

Machine dyeing 80-81
Microcrystalline 24
Mordants 27, 67

Over dyeing 86, 131

Painting with dyes 82-85
Paraffin 12, 23
People in batik 118-119
Photo realism in batik 120-121
Pigment 46
Pointillism 38-39

Resist 12, 14, 99
  cold 24, 30
  commercial 24-25

Salt 27
Setting color 94-96
Sgraffito 23
Site-specific art 117
Sodium alginate 28, 88
Solid areas 33-34, 37
Solvents 28
Stamping tools, *see tjaps*
Still-life in batik 116
Subtractive color 45-46
Synthropol 27

Tjantings 8, 16, 22, 34-35
Tjaps 16, 22-23, 40-41

Urea 27, 74-75, 82

Value 48, 101
Veining 12-13, 33-34

Wax removal 90-93